Pleasure Paradises

Pleasure Paradises

INTERNATIONAL CLUBS AND RESORTS

JOHN P. RADULSKI
WILLIAM WEATHERSBY, JR.

Architecture and
Interior Design Library

AN IMPRINT OF
PBC INTERNATIONAL, INC.

Distributor to the book trade in the United States and Canada
Rizzoli International Publications
through St. Martin's Press
175 Fifth Avenue
New York, NY 10010

Distributor to the art trade in the United States and Canada
PBC International, Inc.
One School Street
Glen Cove, NY 11542

Distributor throughout the rest of the world
Hearst Books International
1350 Avenue of the Americas
New York, NY 10019

Library of Congress Cataloging–in–Publication Data

Radulski, John P.
Pleasure paradises : international clubs and resorts / John P. Radulski, William Weathersby, Jr.
   p.   cm.
  Includes index.
  ISBN 0–86636–496–X   (pbk ISBN 0-86636-536-2)
  1. Hotels—Directories. 2. Resorts—Directories. I. Weathersby, William.
  II. Title.
TX907.R273 1996   96–5730
647.94'025—dc20   CIP

CAVEAT– Information in this text is believed accurate, and will pose no
problem for the student or casual reader. However, the author was often
constrained by information contained in signed release forms, information
that could have been in error or not included at all. Any misinformation
(or lack of information) is the result of failure in these attestations. The
author has done whatever is possible to insure accuracy.

Color separation by C & C Color Graphic Co.
Printing and binding by C & C Offset Printing Co., Ltd.

10 9 8 7 6 5 4 3 2 1

Printed in Hong Kong

To Elizabeth Casey Radulski and other friends and family who long encouraged my often unorthodox spirit of adventure.

JPR

To my parents, William and Charlotte, who taught me early how to travel far and well.

WW

In these pages you will discover a wide array of exciting properties from the mountains to the seas. Each has the distinctive ability to be a pleasure paradise.

A paradise for the turn-of-the century traveler creates an atmosphere of emotional comfort and personal fantasy. The way to a guest's heart is through instant gratification, not delayed action. The promise to make everything perfect must be fulfilled to play out the fantasy; the guest wants comforts anticipated and requests pleasantly and courteously met.

As the global village becomes more intimate and the world of leisure travel grows more sophisticated, we must be evermore caring and responsive. We must make calm reside comfortably with vitality. We must create a luxurious escape from home with all the contentments of home. We must provide both pampered rest and zestful activity—a quiet retreat but not too far from the information highway. Above all we must never be all things to all guests, but all things to each guest.

The voice of a new kind of hospitality must not be rote but warm and personally involved, yet professional in attitude towards meeting the needs of guests. From that initial contact with the person who takes the reservation through your greeting and farewell, recognition and service are the important ingredients of hospitality. Details matter and are noticed.

Today's traveler is knowledgeable and sophisticated with a desire for *la douceur de vivre*—the sweetness of life.

The most discerning are looking for a paradise.

Adriana Mnuchin
The Mayflower Inn
Washington, Connecticut

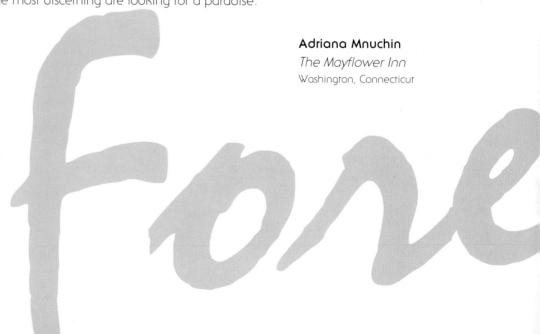

THE GREAT ESCAPE

The world of exploration and adventure has changed considerably since British philosopher Francis Bacon (1561-1626) pronounced that "Travel, in the younger sort, is a part of education; in the elder, a part of experience." Short, easily arranged airline flights today have opened geographically and culturally diverse locales to a wide range of travelers seeking personal growth through leisure, business (state-of-the-art communications in even the most remote resorts can keep you linked to the main office) or both. Similarly, luxury hotels, resorts, spas, country clubs, and cruise ships crafted by world-class interior designers and architects offer elegance and convenience to discriminating sojourners of all ages.

This volume, an all-new sequel to PBC International's *Clubs and Resorts* (published in 1993), showcases the results of an unprecedented surge in new construction and renovation—an international collection of great escapes. Although the projects have been grouped into five separate chapters to focus on each property's main attraction, so to speak, the careful observer will note that there are many features that will encourage making a trek to each pleasure paradise.

The Four Seasons Nevis, for example, is graced with stylish oceanside accommodations in the Caribbean, while avid golfers—representing a growing and affluent market—will marvel at its championship course designed by Robert Trent Jones II to embrace the base of Mt. Nevis. On the other hand, urban spas such as Manhattan's Equinox Club serve as close-to-home daily destinations where the body and spirit can be rejuvenated and refreshed. And for travelers with more expansive schedules and vacation budgets, there are options like the Bühlerhöhe Hotel, which provides a spectacular Black Forest location as well as a diverse choice of athletic-oriented activities and upscale amenities.

Whether your idea of escapism—and exceptional hospitality design—
centers on swinging a six iron, snorkeling past coral reefs, skiing scenic slopes,
climbing across volcanic rocks, setting out on safari, going native in Balinese
dress and attitude, or surfing the World Wide Web on your laptop while
reclining in a palm-shaded hammock, the following facilities will open your
eyes to the latest styles and amenities making waves internationally. We hope
this text will enhance your armchair travel education and experience...at least
until you find time to pack your bags.

John P. Radulski
William Weathersby, Jr.

Exotic

Outposts

BORA BORA LAGOON RESORT

ABOVE *Resort bungalows are grouped in three village-like groups on the island of Motu Toopua.*

ARCHITECT
ARCHITECTURE OCEANIA

INTERIOR DESIGN
ROGER PYKE ARCHITECTURE & INTERIOR DESIGN

PHOTOGRAPHY
COURTESY OF BORA BORA LAGOON RESORT

The Bora Bora Lagoon Resort is a boutique-style property at which 80 bungalows offer guests the highest levels of service and amenities in a tropical setting. Covering approximately 12 oceanside acres on the island of Motu Toopua, the resort comprises campus-like groupings of detached buildings that lend an air of intimacy and exclusivity. Each building reflects the regional "fare" style of design, with wood construction including columns and roof supports hewn from tree trunks and pandanus thatched roofs. So as not to compete with the surrounding natural features, all buildings maintain a low profile. Fifty of the guest bungalows are built on stilts over the lagoon and another 30 are in the tropical gardens and beach location. The bungalows are arranged in three villages, oriented with privacy and views in mind.

The centerpiece of the facility is a clubhouse of sorts, a series of buildings linked by stone walkways. At water's edge is a reception area for guests (each of whom arrives by launch), a library and lounge, lobby, shops, and restaurants. Just outside is a series of terraces. Furnishings are cued by the building itself, with a selection of wicker and rattan seating accented by both subtle and brilliant fabrics. Art and accessories from the area add regional interest.

Dining options include the 60-seat Otemanu Restaurant which serves European, Asian, and American cuisine. An additional 32 patrons can dine on a teak deck above the water. The more casual Cafe Fare seats 68, while poolside is the Hiro Lounge & Bistro. For those craving late-night activity, the Pub Heiva—the resort's only fully enclosed venue constructed underground so as not to disturb other guests—provides a spot for dancing.

ABOVE *Open-air guestrooms showcase the incredible vistas.*
FAR LEFT & LEFT *The local "fare" style of architecture is a perfect backdrop for wicker and rattan furnishings and locally printed textiles.*

LONDOLOZI GAME RESERVE

ABOVE & TOP *The camp's pools and verandas are nestled into the riverside site.*

INTERIOR DESIGN
VISUAL EYES

PHOTOGRAPHY
**COURTESY OF
THE CONSERVATION
CORPORATION**

Originally opened in the 1970s, this recently updated luxury bush lodge is in the heart of the African *bushveld*. The site was a family farm for many years. Four rondavels were originally built, and over the decades the complex has grown to three camps with 24 rooms. Catering to international tourists seeking the adventure of safaris, the lodge features thatched roofs, mosquito-netted bed canopies, rattan furnishings, and many porches and balconies. The main verandas of all three camps are built above the foliage of the local trees, such as the ebony. Eight double chalets with elevated private balconies and in-suite bathrooms nestle into the riverine vegetation overlooking the beautiful Sand River.

The original rustic rondavels offer charming double rooms with in-suite showers and bathrooms. The relaxed Main Camp accommodates 24 guests, and has its own swimming pool, *boma,* and gift shop. The lounge and bar area features a suspended balcony overlooking the river far below, where the clear water cascades over huge granite rocks.

Each guestroom is appointed with locally crafted furniture and artwork, accented by African textiles and rough-hewn details. All large rooms showcase stunning vistas across the riverine bush and beyond, while the outdoor showers afford guests uninterrupted views of hippos, elephants, and other neighborly animals.

ABOVE *An* Out of Africa *ambience
blends British colonial antiques
and regional art, furnishings, and
textiles.*

LEFT *Alfresco dining at the
Londolozi epitomizes a safari feast.*

ABOVE *Mosquito-netted beds and crisp bed linens put an exotic, upscale spin on guests' safari stays.*
OPPOSITE TOP & BOTTOM *Lofty ceilings with exposed thatched roofs and ceiling fans, plus the proximity to native flora and fauna make a Londolozi trip a memorable entry in one's jungle book.*

JEAN-MICHEL COUSTEAU FIJI ISLANDS RESORT

ABOVE & OPPOSITE *The rarely encountered intact tropical forest makes Jean-Michel Cousteau's resort a unique island paradise.*

INTERIOR DESIGN
JANET FREED

PHOTOGRAPHY
JACK DRAFAHL
TOM ORDWAY
STEPHEN PERRY

Jean-Michel Cousteau, son of famed underwater explorer Jacques Cousteau, in 1994 teamed with the owners of Big Sur, California's Post Ranch Inn to acquire this resort overlooking Savusavu Bay on Vanua Levu, one of more than 300 Fiji Islands. Previously managed by an Australian company, the enclave was home for five years to Jean-Michel's Project Ocean Search, an undersea education program. Though he did not consider himself a hotelier, Cousteau saw the potential in the operation and couldn't pass it up since he didn't want to lose access to the rarely encountered intact tropical forests and healthy reefs.

Situated on 17 acres on Lesiaceva Point, which stretches into the Koro Sea, the resort comprises a row of 12 thatched-roof guest bures, or Fijian bungalows, with waterfront views, eight more bures behind those, a main lodge bure with open-air bar and restaurant, snorkeling and training facilities, and volleyball and tennis courts. A bure designed solely for children is planned.

Nestled within a coconut grove, the spacious guest bures feature 30-foot-high ceilings, ceiling fans, and comfortable furnishings selected by designer Janet Freed. Each bure is decorated with wicker and rattan furnishings and local timbers, complementing the palette of green, red, and tan cued by hues of the local banana leaf. A frog motif, inspired as a tribute to "frogman" Cousteau, is carried throughout the decor, from a frog depicted on a single tile in every bathroom to the cut-outs in the metal tabletops of the bar.

The resort features a seaside pool that flows through the restaurant and bar, while amenities include evening turndown, laundry, in-room massage therapy, and a conference room accommodating 40 persons.

Cousteau and his partners are balancing the need for first-rate accommodations with the challenge of maintaining the natural environment. Conservation precautions afford guests the continuing opportunity to experience the main show here—viewing the unspoiled wonders of the sea.

ABOVE *Guest bures feature slat blinds, ceiling fans, 30-foot ceilings, and upscale furnishings with a Fijian flair.*

FAR LEFT & LEFT *Evening turndown and in-room massage therapy are amenities. Local timbers and thatched roofs create a scenic spot for lounging on the porch of a guest bure.*

Nusa Dua Beach Hotel

ABOVE *A new pool outfitted with special chemical-free filteration enhances the resort's outdoor amenities.*

Situated on the southern peninsula of Bali, this recently renovated and upgraded hotel is minutes away from the Ngurah International Airport and within easy traveling distance to the island's attractions. The resort comprises 335 guestrooms, 45 suites, five restaurants, four bars, tennis and squash courts, and a full-service spa. Built with Balinese style architectural features including open-air lounges, terraced gardens, and carved wooden shutters, the hotel is filled with furnishings that also showcase the skill of local artisans. The lobby has been transformed to provide a more spacious feeling, better access, and a grander welcome while retaining the vernacular ambience. A new lagoon-shaped swimming pool fringed with white sand has two small islands at its center as well as special chemical-free filtration.

For guestrooms, the 30-square-meters superior rooms feature parquet flooring with tumbled-marble borders, private balconies, and Balinese-style furnishings. Deluxe rooms measure 38 square meters and have shutters embellished with Balinese woodcarving. Palace Lanai rooms are 45 square meters with private balconies leading to landscaped gardens. A Palace Lounge and 24-hour butler service are additional amenities.

Besides the array of bars and restaurants—which range from an Italian cafe to an alfresco spa cafe under the banyan trees—a 380-seat traditional Balinese open-air theater presents classical cultural performances accompanied by buffet dinners.

ARCHITECT
PEDDLE THORP ARCHITECT

INTERIOR DESIGN
JULIE ACKLAND

PHOTOGRAPHY
COURTESY OF NUSA DUA BEACH HOTEL

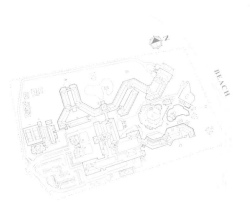

BEACH

ABOVE *Balinese carvings and tropical plantings grace an outdoor terrace.*

LEFT *Refurbished guestrooms feature Balinese batik prints and locally crafted furnishings.*

MOWANA SAFARI LODGE

ABOVE *Visitors to the Mowana Safari Lodge are encouraged to explore the land and waterways that surround the facility.*

ABOVE RIGHT *The lodge comprises a series of buildings located along the riverbank.*

ARCHITECT
AFRICA INTERNATIONAL DESIGN & PROJECT SERVICES

INTERIOR DESIGN
PROFURN CONTRACTS

PHOTOGRAPHY
SACHI & SACHI

The Mowana Safari Lodge was designed to immerse guests in an African wilderness experience. Within the trappings of five-star accommodations and services, visitors are encouraged to sample the unique opportunities found in a spot where hippos, crocodiles, and other fauna are neighbors. The owner worked very closely with government agencies to assure that there would be minimal changes to the landscape and that animals would be able to walk the banks of the fronting river.

The result is a central, pod-like facility housing the reception area, restaurant, conference room, cocktail lounge, and office space. Inside, traditional art and artifacts purchased from a number of artisans in Africa's southern regions are used extensively.

The two guestroom wings extend from the central building, their footprints following irregular paths around existing trees on the property. In-room design features include wicker chairs and tables that complement the wooden grounds outdoors. Air conditioning, mosquito netting, ceiling fans, mini-bars, and hair dryers in each room add a home-like, comfortable ambience.

Individuals and groups are afforded a variety of programs to help them learn about the regional culture and wildlife. Educational films are screened three times per day and professional guides are available to lead fishing expeditions and bird and animal watching trips. The Mowana staff will pack gourmet lunches to be served during game drives, and sunset cruises along the river make the idea of "roughing it" quite attractive.

ABOVE *Vibrantly colored fabrics add flair in the dining room, a central meeting place for guests.*
LEFT *Well-appointed guestrooms feature a comfortable blend of rattan seating and casegoods.*

Le Touessrok Hotel & Il-Aux-Cerfs

A recent $26-million upgrade and expansion of a favorite destination in the Indian Ocean for European travelers has turned Le Touessrok Hotel and the adjoining Il-Aux-Cerfs into an idyllic first-class property. Addressed during the project was the redesign of the lobby and other public areas including two restaurants, refurbishment of 100 guestrooms, the construction of 38 junior suites and a presidential suite, and softgoods renovation of 60 standard rooms.

Le Touessrok is centered around a two-story reception building that was opened up to take advantage of the natural and man-made water features within the resort. In the lobby, the design team used batik prints, rattan furniture, and millwork to conjure a look reminiscent of a private residence. Upstairs is La Passarelle, a 400-seat dining room. As in other public areas, upholstery and other fabrics based on the vibrant hues found in native flowers are a bright touch. Outside this building is a large swimming pool, its perimeter dotted with thatch-roofed pavilions that serve as open-air lounges and bars.

A relaxed yet stylish ambience is achieved in the guestrooms, mixing the design influences of India as well as those imported by the Dutch, British, and French who originally came to the island to raise sugar cane. Locally crafted casegoods, rattan pieces, and accessories are unified through carefully selected fabrics that bring indoors the tropical colors found in the landscape.

The Il-Aux-Cerfs portion of the resort is located on a small island reached via a footbridge. Here, the 54-seat La Veranda restaurant serves Italian fare in an indoor-outdoor setting among the clustered low-rise buildings housing guestrooms.

ABOVE *Luxuriant plantings are arranged along a meandering series of new swimming pools and other water features.*

OPPOSITE *Newel posts in the shape of pineapples are integrated into the stairway that links the reception building's two levels.*

ARCHITECT
MAURICE GIRAUD

INTERIOR DESIGN
WILSON & ASSOCIATES

PHOTOGRAPHY
MIKE WILSON

BELOW *Quilted coverlets in bright tropical colors enliven the guestrooms, while marble flooring adds another elegant touch. Sliding louvered screens permit easy control of light.*

ABOVE *A private terrace, part of each of the 38 newly built junior suites, is a relaxing place for guests to dine or entertain.*

LEFT *The luxurious appointments found in each guestroom continue into the marble-clad bathrooms.*

LEFT *Le Sega Bar, set among the series of pools, features a mix of wood building materials and finishes. The domed ceiling is a dramatic design element.*

BELOW *Thatch-roofed pavilions house lounges and other out-of-the-sun facilities at the resort.*

BOTTOM *A sophisticated lighting scheme adds romance to La Veranda restaurant at the Il-Aux-Cerfs component of the resort.*

SHERATON INN AT TIMIKA

ABOVE *Reception, dining, and other function areas are located within a multistory lodge building.*
ABOVE RIGHT *Wood carvings crafted by local tribes are placed both inside and on the grounds of the resort.*
OPPOSITE *A large window wall framed by decoratively carved columns rises to the full height of the reception lobby.*

ARCHITECT/INTERIOR DESIGN
HELLMUTH, OBATA & KASSABAUM, INC.

PHOTOGRAPHY
NICK MERRICK

In 1990, P.T. Freeport Indonesia, a copper mining operation, hired Hellmuth, Obata, & Kassabaum to master-plan a town for 30,000 that would provide accommodations for Freeport employees and their families, as well as visitors including government officials. One component of this "New Town" is the Sheraton Inn at Timika, designed and constructed with unwavering attention to the site's location adjacent to a rain forest.

The property comprises a main lodge with a reception and lobby area, 120-seat restaurant, bar, meeting rooms, and a fitness center arranged on the main floor. A grand, double staircase leads to an upper level, from which a series of multiunit guestroom pavilions with accommodations for 84 (a 100-guestroom expansion is planned) are reached via above-ground walkways wending around existing flora.

A strong sense of place is established within the entrance lobby, where Indonesian woods and marble plus other stone materials add a rich, textural finish to the space. All of the furnishings, including fabrics, were designed and produced in a variety of Indonesian locations. Throughout the hotel, an extensive array of local paintings, textiles, antiques, and artifacts are on display. Included are wood carvings—produced by members of the Komoro and Asmat tribes—that range from small interior accent pieces to 10-foot-tall statues in the bar and entry garden.

LEFT *Refined furnishings in the lodge, such as these seating groups, afford comfortable surroundings.*
BELOW *The dining room is defined by sponged wall treatments and a series of locally carved wall panels.*
OPPOSITE *Coffered wall panels set a comfortable visual rhythm balanced by that of the balustrades in the lobby.*

ABOVE *Elevated walkways link the lodge with a series of guestroom buildings to lessen environmental impact.*

ABOVE & LEFT *The majority of fabrics in guestrooms was woven locally, although all the furniture came from suppliers in the region.*

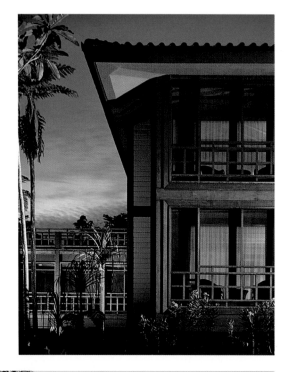

RIGHT & BELOW *Attention to craftsmanship is evidenced in the architectural style throughout the resort.*

FAR RIGHT *Shaded seating areas dot the pool area.*

COSTA CAREYES, MEXICO

HOTEL BEL-AIR
COSTA CAREYES

Pure pleasure and relaxation are offered at the Hotel Bel-Air Costa Careyes, a 60-guestroom resort located about 120 miles south of Puerto Vallarta. Here, public areas and guest units are built right at the edge of the Pacific Ocean's "Turtle Coast" to make the most of spectacular views.

To further relate interior and exterior spaces, solid walls are used only where absolutely necessary, and open-air pavilions and lanais abound. Guestrooms, for example, have natural terracotta floor tiles and are sparsely yet decoratively furnished for clean-lined comfort. Crisp white walls are punched with wide windows and doorways that lead to private, covered patios with plunge pools. Similarly outfitted are the 110-seat main restaurant and the popular Terrace Bistro, from which diners can watch the sun set over the Pacific. The menu includes Italian, Mexican, and tropical-influenced fare.

Though the emphasis at Costa Careyes is on leisure, a suite of conference salons caters to groups of up to 100 persons. Athletically inclined guests can also take advantage of an equestrian center, tennis courts, water-related activities, and a 3,500-square-foot health, fitness, and beauty spa.

TOP & ABOVE *The Hotel Bel-Air Costa Careyes is located among the natural splendors of the Pacific Ocean.*

OPPOSITE *Stands of native palm trees are set within the free-form swimming pool accented by brightly colored mosaic tiles.*

ARCHITECT/INTERIOR DESIGN
PLAN ARQUITECTOS

PHOTOGRAPHY
MILROY & MCALEER

Guestrooms, comfortably appointed with regionally inspired furnishings, were designed with generously scaled openings to the outdoors.

High in

the Hills

ARCHITECT
**URBAN DESIGN
GROUP, INC.**

INTERIOR DESIGN
WILSON & ASSOCIATES

PHOTOGRAPHY
R. GREG HURSLEY, INC.

LAKE BUENA VISTA, FLORIDA

DISNEY'S WILDERNESS LODGE

The 728-guestroom Disney's Wilderness Lodge, although located in the sprawling Walt Disney World complex, presents elaborately handcrafted interiors that recall such historic lodges as the Old Faithful Inn at Yellowstone National Park built almost 100 years ago. The 510,000-square-foot building is clad with natural log veneer over steel-and-concrete for an appropriately rustic look. Enhancing the effect, the grounds are planted with stands of birch, pine, oak, and cedar trees interspersed with water features including a geyser.

In the six-story lobby, columns formed from bundled logs rise the full height and support the open-beam ceiling. Metal and glass chandeliers reinterpret the look and decorative patterns found on teepees. A three-story fireplace with a chimney reaching to the roof is constructed of piled rocks and commands one corner of the room. The soaring verticality of the lobby is tempered by wood railings that separate the guestroom-floor corridors from the atrium on all four sides.

Leather and richly toned woven fabrics with patterns inspired by Native American textiles dress the lounge chairs, rockers, and settees, which all carry out an Arts & Crafts aesthetic. Area rugs, reminiscent of the woven fabrics in coloration and pattern, are set atop a floor that combines cherry, white oak, bird's-eye maple, and burl walnut. Similar materials and styles carry into the adjacent one-level registration area, and a cozy library and the Whispering Canyon Cafe accessed from the atrium lobby.

ABOVE *A window wall in the Wilderness Lodge lobby frames views of the lushly landscaped grounds.*

OPPOSITE *The atrium lobby rises six stories. Glowing teepee-topped chandeliers are suspended from rough-hewn log rafters.*

LEFT *Full-service dining is offered in the Whispering Canyon Cafe located adjacent to the registration area. Materials and design elements echo those in the atrium lobby, but on a reduced scale.*

LEFT *Quiet and cozy, the library is a popular spot for reading up on the history of the West. The artwork here, as in other areas of the resort, celebrates the magnificence of that quintessentially American region.*

POST RANCH INN

BIG SUR, CALIFORNIA

ABOVE *Decks along the steep cliffs provide sweeping views of the Pacific.*

ARCHITECT
G.K. MICKEY MUENNIG

INTERIOR DESIGN
JANET GAY FREED

PHOTOGRAPHY
LARRY DALE GORDON

The 30 private guest houses of the Post Ranch Inn in Big Sur, a cliffside enclave between Los Angeles and San Francisco, overlook the Pacific Ocean. Built on almost 100 acres owned by the Post family, who have been residents of the area since the mid-1800s, the inn continues the tradition of preserving the natural surroundings. The actual site played a major part in the design, since architect Mickey Muennig is a long-time Big Sur resident and worked with the natural terrain he was given. "The magnificent sea cliffs, mountains, and trees were already in place; it was up to me to fill in the spaces with the elements as natural and peaceful as the land," he says. The resort is designed "for people to feel a part of nature, not merely to be observers of it."

The inn houses a complete spa with a full-time staff, and is home to the renowned Sierra Mar restaurant, with its beautiful bar and a small library featuring historical Big Sur books and artifacts. A basking pool and lap pool offer spectacular views.

There are four architectural styles among the 30 units: Ocean Houses, located on the ridge with sod roofs; Tree Houses built on stilts to protect the shallow redwood tree roots; Coast Houses and Mountain Houses that are cylindrical in shape; and tri-level Butterfly Houses. Local materials used in the architectural design include slate, wood, and stone.

The private guest houses feature fireplaces, expansive windows, mini bars, state-of-the-art music systems, large custom spa tubs, and the option of in-room massages by a member of the spa staff. Besides massages, guests can enjoy facials, yoga, and aerobics classes. There are also nature hikes in the surrounding hills and stargazing through a powerful telescope.

ABOVE *The architect, a longtime resident of Big Sur, carefully plotted the inn so as not to disturb the natural terrain.*

LEFT *Alfresco dining delivers a dramatic vista.*

TOP *The Post Ranch Inn's spa-style bathrooms also put the land-scape at center stage.*

ABOVE *The cliff-side Sierra Mar restaurant is a perfect place to watch the sun set over the Pacific.*

RIGHT *Expanses of glass bring the views indoors. Fireplaces and wood beams add a casual, beachcomber ambience.*

WYOMING INN

Like many other resorts in the Rockies, the Wyoming Inn of Jackson Hole caters to both leisure and business travelers seeking comfort among the region's natural splendors. The proximity of the Wyoming Inn to the center of the town's historic district placed great import on creating a non-obtrusive scale for the building while tying it visually to its surroundings. The inn rises only three stories high in its two-acre site. Its facades are layered, starting off with a base of stone veneer for a hefty, substantial look, with upper levels clad in red cedar. Ornate timber trusses support the porte cochere that leads to a pair of glass entry doors etched with depictions of deer and elk. A variety of artisans including locals were tapped to create the decorative elements within the hotel, such as the doors and the face of the reception desk graced with reliefs of an elk and a bighorn sheep.

A focal attraction in the lobby is a chandelier made of moose horns suspended from the coffered wood ceiling. The intricate millwork continues around the room and at one end sheathes a double-height arched alcove surrounding a stone fireplace. The room is centered by a large, multicolored hand-made area rug from China.

Many of the guestrooms include fireplaces, fully-equipped kitchenettes, and whirlpool tubs. The motifs inspired by nature and found in the inn's public spaces are rendered in fabrics for bedspreads and drapery treatments in these private retreats.

ABOVE *The three-story facade of the inn is clad in stone veneer and red cedar, with a timber-trussed porte cochere.*
OPPOSITE *Glass entry doors are etched with depictions of deer and elk.*

ARCHITECT
ARCHITECTS VAN LOM/ EDWARDS, AIA, PC

INTERIOR DESIGN
TOM LYONS MCCLASKEY ENTERPRISES

PHOTOGRAPHY
HEIDI A. DAVIS

ABOVE *Rustic decorative motifs found in the inn's public spaces are continued in the guestrooms.*

LEFT *A chandelier made of moose horns is suspended from the coffered wood ceiling in the lobby.*

BRASSTOWN VALLEY

Owned by the State of Georgia, Brasstown Valley was developed by Stormont Trice Corporation as a conference center in the remote North Georgia Mountains to help stimulate the local economy. The 504-acre resort includes an 18-hole golf course, tennis courts, hiking trails, undeveloped woodlands, and fishing streams. Environmental sensitivity was a high priority, and the developer had to obtain 16 environmental-related permits during construction.

The great room of the hexagonal lodge building evokes a rustic ambience with a 72-foot-high stone fireplace, heavy wood beams, and extensive woodwork. Georgia white pine walls in a Pickwick pattern complement wide-plank, yellow pine floors and rustic hickory and laurel railings. Tree trunks support the balcony over the front desk area. The designers modulated the amount of wood by using a three-color stain system: walls are the lightest color, the floor and ceiling are of medium value, and beam casings and baseboards the darkest shade. Windows overlook the golf course and mountains beyond.

In the main living areas, the furnishings, artwork, and accessories were selected for a "collected" look. The designers were asked to use as many Georgia resources as possible, so local woodworkers and artists were commissioned to make cabinets, tables, a grandfather's clock, benches, and coat stands. A variety of overstuffed sofas and chairs in rich fabrics and leathers are set amid wingback wicker chairs and hickory game chairs. Custom antler chandeliers complete the scheme, which is carried through to the 175-seat restaurant and bar.

ABOVE *The main lodge building overlooks the golf course and surrounding mountains.*
OPPOSITE *A towering stone fireplace dominates the hexagonal great room.*

ARCHITECT
COOPER CARRY ARCHITECTS

INTERIOR DESIGN
MARCIA DAVIS & ASSOCIATES, INC.

PHOTOGRAPHY
BENZUR ARCHITECTURAL PHOTOGRAPHY INC.; JOE STEWARDSON

OPPOSITE & LEFT *Railings and columns created from local hickory and laurel trees are a rustic touch.*

BELOW LEFT *Many of the lodge's furnishings were crafted by local artisans.*

BELOW RIGHT *Cozy bedrooms open out onto porches or terraces.*

THE PEAKS AT TELLURIDE

ABOVE & TOP *The San Juan Mountains envelop The Peaks at Telluride.*

INTERIOR DESIGN
ZIMMER HUNDLEY ASSOCIATES

PHOTOGRAPHY
COURTESY OF THE PEAKS

The Peaks at Telluride sits at 9,500 feet and is ringed by the San Juan Mountains that rise to a spectacular height of 14,000 feet. This setting was embraced by the resort's design team, who worked to take advantage of the views now offered throughout the year from public areas and all 177 guestrooms—including 28 suites.

A series of recent enhancements has freshened the resort's aesthetic appeal. The lobby, with heavy rough-hewn timbers, an oversized stone fireplace, and stone flooring, is filled with furniture, art, textiles and other design elements from the region for a comfortable mix of the rustic and refined.

One of the main meeting places is the 130-seat Legends of the Peaks restaurant, where meals are served indoors throughout the day. An adjacent 35-seat brick-paved deck offers seating during all seasons. A lobby bar serves light snacks and libations.

Business and social functions are accommodated among four meeting rooms and a 2,100-square-foot ballroom. On-site recreational activities center around a 42,000-square-foot spa spread over four levels. Forty-four treatment rooms afford a range of body treatments. Saunas, steam rooms, an indoor/outdoor pool, weight rooms, racquet sport courts, and an indoor climbing wall are all included here. Guests can also enjoy an 18-hole golf course that is sited alongside the resort.

ABOVE *The fireplace and flooring made of stone complement rustic and refined furnishings in the lobby.*

FAR LEFT *A heated outdoor pool makes all seasons in Colorado a scenic pleasure.*

LEFT *The 130-seat Legends of the Peaks is a popular meeting place.*

THE LITTLE NELL

ABOVE & TOP *Part of the skiing hub set at the base of Aspen Mountain, The Little Nell features pointed gables and pronounced setbacks to echo the lines of the terrain.*

ARCHITECT
HAGMAN YAW ARCHITECTS

INTERIOR DESIGN
ANN MILLIGAN GRAY

PHOTOGRAPHY
DAVE MARLOW PHOTOGRAPHY

The Aspen Skiing Company operates three of its namesake region's more popular destination resorts: The Aspen Meadows, The Snowmass Lodge & Club, and The Little Nell. Each offers a wealth of four-season recreational and cultural activities, yet it is The Little Nell, just steps from the base of Aspen Mountain, that has become the in-town meeting place for media moguls and other high-profile international visitors looking for attentive service in the area's most elegantly appointed lodging spot.

The Little Nell is only four levels high and, with its carefully articulated facades, was designed to present a face sympathetic to the area's geography: pointed gables and pronounced setbacks echo the undulating mountains. Landscaping smoothes the transition to the adjacent, upmarket shopping district of downtown Aspen.

The mountain motif is maintained throughout the interiors of the 92-guestroom hotel. In the lobby, fashioned as a cozy living room, Colorado granite frames the double-sided fireplace that reaches from floor to ceiling. Belgian wool carpets atop sandstone floors set the stage for down-filled sofas. Another popular gathering place is the oak-paneled library—available for private functions of up to 30 people—which overlooks the 140-seat restaurant serving American cuisine and spotlighting local fare. Other private and public spots include three meeting rooms and an outdoor dining terrace. Also outdoors is a heated swimming pool and whirlpool spa, though indoors are steam and massage rooms in addition to exercise facilities.

Guestrooms, including 13 suites, continue the luxurious comfort found on The Little Nell's main floor. Each room has views of the town or the mountain. Imported area rugs and oversized beds and seating pieces guarantee comfort, as do fireplaces. Marble-lined bathrooms are standard.

All guests may enjoy 24-hour room service, while winter visitors are afforded a ski concierge who facilitates the hotel's ski-in/ski-out location by providing such services as ski tuning and waxing.

ABOVE & LEFT Guestrooms continue the casual theme, with mountain views prominently showcased. Fireplaces, comfortable furnishings, and lofty ceilings impart a residential ambience.

ABOVE & TOP *Woodlands and lush gardens surround the country estate-like Lodge at Koele.*

LANA'I, HAWAII
LODGE AT KOELE

The 102-guestroom lodge is nestled amid the central highlands of Lana'i, Hawaii's sixth-largest island. At 1,600 feet above sea level, the retreat takes its name from the nearby farming region that lies above Lana'i City, the island's only town. The lodge is one of the rare inland hotels in Hawaii, surrounded by groves of pine, banyan, eucalyptus, jacaranda, and a series of lush formal gardens appointed with charming and serene Asian stone carvings. It resembles a grand estate or country lodge, with heavy timbers, high-beamed ceilings, and massive stone fireplaces. Architectural details emphasize comfort and turn-of-the-century, old world elegance.

The Great Hall, filled with an extensive collection of Pacific art and artifacts, leads to a spectacular porch, the perfect setting for afternoon tea. A library, music room, and trophy room continue the ambience of a plantation home. Guests dine in the formal octagonal dining room, that features a fireplace, or on the adjacent terrace open to the outside and offering views of the hillside gardens.

Activities at the lodge include croquet, lawn bowling, horseback riding, jeep rides, swimming, tennis, garden walks, and golf.

ARCHITECT
THE LANAI CO., INC.

INTERIOR DESIGN
JOSZI MESKAN

PHOTOGRAPHY
JEFFREY ASHER

LEFT *With wicker furnishings and a row of French doors, the porch is the perfect spot for a respite.*
BELOW *The spacious guestrooms at the Lodge are casual yet elegant.*

THE MAYFLOWER INN

ABOVE *The main house's wide porch provides a genteel setting for drinks or conversation.*
TOP *The gambrel-roofed inn overlooks one of the many gardens on the grounds.*
OPPOSITE *A stairway lined with antique portraits defines the main lobby.*

ARCHITECT
THORNE & CLEAVES

INTERIOR DESIGN
GOMEZ ASSOCIATES

PHOTOGRAPHY
**JOHN KANE
COURTESY OF
THE MAYFLOWER INN**

Standing on the site of a private school built in the late 1800s, The Mayflower Inn offers guests an urbane and sophisticated retreat just two hours northeast of New York City. The gambrel-roofed building, clad in white clapboards on its lower level and gray-green ones on the upper two, easily fits in with the vernacular architectural styles of the region. Inside, the furnishings lend a unique and far-from-generic appeal.

The double-height entrance lobby previews the extensive array of 18th and 19th century art and antiques collected by the owners in the U.S. and Europe and displayed throughout the 28,000-square-foot property. Persian carpets cover wood plank flooring, while seating fabrics range from heavy floral tapestries to subtle geometrics. A stairway lined with antique oil portraits hugs one side of the room. Flanking the lobby, a cozy library to one side and a living-room-style lounge on the other continue the subdued palette.

To the rear of the lobby, a bar, main dining room, and private dining room are coordinated with dark green-painted walls and complementary plaid draperies. Windows frame views across the inn's south lawn and the forested Berkshires.

The larger building contains 15 guestrooms including four suites, with nine additional guestrooms distributed between two other buildings. Each room features a different color scheme and is furnished with antique and reproduction casegoods and seating pieces. Fireplaces and balconies are common amenities.

ABOVE LEFT *Large bathrooms with double sinks, walnut wainscotting, limoges fittings and tapestry mats complete the setting and enhance the inn's guest lodgings.*

RIGHT *Each room is individually decorated with antique English desks and other traditional furnishings amassed by the owners—giving Mayflower the look of a private home.*

ABOVE RIGHT *An antique sleigh-bed enhanced with a hand-made quilt graces this junior suite which overlooks Mayflower Mountain and its hiking trails.*

Also on the grounds is the restored Teahouse outfitted for private meetings and social functions, an outdoor swimming pool surrounded by a stone terrace, and tennis courts. Hundreds of feet of old stone walls have been preserved along the 28 acres, and the native trees and shrubs on site are accented by formal gardens and rare specimen trees.

ABOVE *The heated swimming pool is nestled in the meticulously manicured grounds. The fine old trees of New England add grandeur to the setting.*

Paradise

COBBLERS COVE
ST. PETER, BARBADOS, WEST INDIES

HYATT REGENCY COOLUM INTERNATIONAL
RESORT & SPA
COOLUM BEACH, AUSTRALIA

EL CONQUISTADOR RESORT & COUNTRY CLUB
LAS CROABAS, PUERTO RICO

FOUR SEASONS RESORT NEVIS
NEVIS, WEST INDIES

ATLANTIS
PARADISE ISLAND, BAHAMAS

CELEBRITY CENTURY
PORT OF CALL, FORT LAUDERDALE, FLORIDA

CARNIVAL CRUISE LINES IMAGINATION
PORT OF CALL, MIAMI, FLORIDA

ROYAL CARIBBEAN LEGEND OF THE SEAS
PORT OF CALL, MIAMI, FLORIDA

by the Water

COBBLERS COVE

Blending the elegance and charm of an English country estate with the tropical beauty and character of the Caribbean, the intimate Cobblers Cove offers just 40 suites and an atmosphere that the management likens to a genteel house party. The pink stucco main house was originally built as a seaside home for the Haynes family, who owned a number of sugar plantations in Barbados. Converted to a hotel in 1986 and recently refurbished, the colonial guest house ambience is enhanced by an extensive use of chintz and furnishings with classic lines. The English country ethos is furthered by the clientele, 75 percent of which comprises travelers from the United Kingdom.

Intimate and comfortable, the suites are tastefully decorated to make guests feel at home and pampered at the same time. Arranged in two-story bungalows around well tended gardens, the suites each feature an air-conditioned bedroom, bathroom, kitchenette, and living area that opens onto a terrace or balcony. For ultimate hideaways, two specialty suites in the main house, the Camelot and the Colleton, are each graced with a four-poster bed, private plunge pool, and rooftop terrace with a view of the Caribbean.

The poolside bar serves refreshing drinks while the terrace restaurant presents award-winning, international cuisine prepared by French-trained chefs

ARCHITECT
IAN MORRISON ASSOCIATES

INTERIOR DESIGN
PRUE LANE FOX

PHOTOGRAPHY
LARSEN COLLINGE INTERNATIONAL

ABOVE *A tree-lined stretch of beach is available to guests. The resort can also arrange a variety of water-oriented activities.*

OPPOSITE *The facade of the resort's main house features curved bays and a vibrant pink stucco finish.*

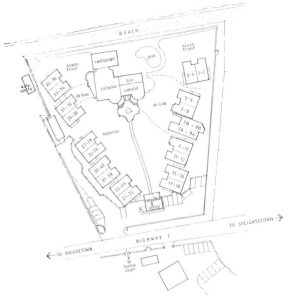

ABOVE A pair of guestroom bungalows is located
beside the main house for easy pool access.
LEFT A living room in the main house displays a
decidedly British aesthetic.
OPPOSITE The interiors of the resort maintain the
elegant appointments of its days as a
private residence.

using fresh local produce and seafood. Exchange arrangements with

varied upscale hotels nearby allow guests to wander further afield to exper-

ience other menu offerings. For the more energetic, Cobblers Cove provides

complimentary tennis, water skiing, windsurfing, sailing, and snorkeling. Other

leisure activities, such as deep sea fishing, parasailing, cricket, polo, sightsee-

ing, and evening cocktail cruises, can be easily arranged.

ABOVE *Folding louvered panels in this bungalow guestroom open to a covered porch.*

RIGHT *Comfort is key in guestrooms, with ceiling fans installed to augment the ocean breezes.*

OPPOSITE *The sparkling blue water of the pool matches that of the vibrant sea beyond.*

Hyatt Regency Coolum International Resort & Spa

ABOVE An Australian rain forest setting rich in natural resources enhances the environment of the Hyatt Regency Coolum.

OPPOSITE The indigenous architecture of Queensland inspired this tiled porte cochere entry to the resort and spa.

ARCHITECT
Bligh Jessup Robinson Pty. Ltd.

DESIGN CONSULTANTS
Wimberly Allison Tong & Goo; Hirsch/Bedner Associates

PHOTOGRAPHY
Berger/Conser

On a 370-acre site encompassing lush rainforest and almost a mile of Pacific beach, a sprawling executive retreat in Queensland helps guests to wind down and shape up. Rather than housing visitors in a main building, the Hyatt Regency Coolum resort is laid out in a decentralized village plan. Villas and suites are scattered in clusters, with each group serviced by a central lounge where breakfast and cocktails are served. There are 150 two-bedroom President's Club villas, 18 two-bedroom and six three-bedroom Ambassador's Club villas, and 156 Regency Club suites. Some units are operated as time-shares. Three main guest clubs are set amid a fitness spa, golf and tennis facilities, and a village square restaurant hub.

The look of the outlying buildings was inspired by the vernacular architecture of the region. Cottages are geared toward the hot climate, with verandas, porches, louvered doors, pitched roofs, and trellises. Exposed indigenous woods, stucco, and metal roofs keep the look unpretentious.

Carrying the theme indoors, color palettes are keyed to the surroundings. Oversize wicker and rough-hewn wood furnishings complement stone and stucco surfaces, print fabrics, clay tile floors, and works by local artists.

With its own medical director, the fitness and health management facility offers aerobics and an exercise gym, lap pool and hydrotherapy, diagnostic medical/health area, squash courts, and separate spas for men and women. Whirlpools, saunas, and beauty treatment areas are part of the center. An adjacent conference center houses two main conference rooms, four meeting rooms, and 18 smaller function rooms.

LEFT *The reception lobby highlights the work of local artisans within a casual, rough-hewn decor.*

OPPOSITE *Roomy wicker chairs and expanses of glass create a connection to the beautiful surroundings in one resort dining and lounging spot.*

ABOVE *Latticework, a pitched metal roof, and wood porches distinguish the vernacular architecture of the guest bungalows.*

LEFT *Alfresco breakfast dining upon a Coolum terrace offers spectacular views Down Under.*

EL CONQUISTADOR RESORT & COUNTRY CLUB

Following about 30 years of success and failure, a resort set on the cliffs overlooking the Atlantic Ocean and Caribbean Sea was closed for a $250-million revitalization program that has resulted in the El Conquistador Resort & Country Club, encompassing more than one million square feet of space.

The design team collaborated to create four distinct guest components that embrace Mediterranean-style design features for a unified look. The main building contains 530 guestrooms. Nearby is Las Casitas Village, a group of 90 detached and attached units. Las Olas Village comprises 73 deluxe suites, while at ocean level is the 144-guestroom La Marina Village.

The main building is a social center for guests in all four areas and houses the vast majority of public facilities: a convention center, casino space, shopping arcade, lounges and nightclubs, and a wealth of restaurants offering a choice of almost everything from Japanese to local gourmet cuisine.

Recreational amenities are centered around a 1.5-acre outdoor aquatics center adjacent to the main building where three swimming pools, whirlpool spas, and other water features appeal to guests of all ages. The site also has a golf course and tennis courts. And just a short boat ride away, the 100-acre, resort-owned Palomino Island enhances swimming and other water sports options.

ABOVE *Crisply delineated groupings of columns surround a whirlpool spa at the center of the resort's 1.5-acre aquatics center.*

RIGHT *Designer Jorge Rossello selected a variety of artwork, including this sculpture, to accent both indoor and outdoor areas.*

OPPOSITE *The resort's aquatics center is used for sport and resort-wide and private functions.*

ARCHITECT
EDWARD DURELL STONE & ASSOCIATES

INTERIOR DESIGN
JORGE ROSSELLO AND ASSOCIATES INTERIOR DESIGNERS-SPACE PLANNERS

PHOTOGRAPHY
**MILROY/MCALEER
RICARDO GUERRA**

RIGHT *During the renovation and expansion of the property, walls that previously prevented views of the landscape and ocean were replaced by windows. Brightly patterned fabrics enliven this seating area near the main reception desk.*

BELOW RIGHT *A fountain in the three-level lobby leading to the conference center brings the sight and sound of water indoors.*

ABOVE & OPPOSITE *The fluid lines of sculpture are a contemporary counterpoint to the angular geometric details of the main building at El Conquistador.*

OPPOSITE & ABOVE *A common feature in guestroom units is sliding louvered doors that open to a private terrace or balcony. The furnishings combine wood seating and casegoods with focal rugs atop marble flooring.*

LEFT & BELOW *Vibrantly hued ceramic tiles are freely used throughout the property.*

FOUR SEASONS RESORT NEVIS

ABOVE *Public areas and guestroom units at the Four Seasons Resort Nevis are clustered in low-slung beachside buildings.*

INTERIOR DESIGN
THE SWA GROUP

PHOTOGRAPHY
JOY VON TIEDEMANN

Although the Four Seasons Resort Nevis caters to incentive and business travelers—there are 5,000 square feet of dedicated meeting areas on site—the majority of guests come to relax, a fact underscored by a full-range of recreational facilities. Amenities include a recently expanded pool area, a 2,000-foot stretch of beach and a range of water sport opportunities, a Robert Trent Jones II championship golf course, 10 tennis courts, and a health club. Island excursions also can be easily arranged.

The architecture and interior design of the resort reinforce the informal yet rarified lifestyle adopted by guests. All buildings—including guestroom cottages and a central, lodge-style Great House with restaurants, lounges, and commons areas—have low articulated rooflines that rise no higher that the surrounding groves of palm trees. Indigenous materials and construction methods present a timeless look in keeping with historic island residences and public buildings.

Foodservice facilities include the open-air Grill Room; the Dining Room, Library, and Tap Room in the Great House; and the poolside Ocean Terrace. Each venue offers local fruits, vegetables, and seafood prepared in a variety of ways, especially showcasing dishes of the West Indies.

Guestrooms range in size from 550 to 2,200 square feet and are outfitted in island-influenced Four Seasons style. Wood casegoods, rattan seating, regional artwork, and fine, muted toned fabrics accented by bright tropical colors all enhance the luxurious, private domain.

ABOVE & LEFT *Guestroom decor achieves a pleasing balance between elegance and island comfort.*

ATLANTIS

A recent investment of close to $250 million allowed Sun International to purchase three resort properties on Paradise Island, which the company has renovated and refurbished. The largest, now called Atlantis, houses close to 1,100 guestrooms.

The name Atlantis is apt since the property overlooks white-sand beaches and is situated among a new 14-acre water park comprising fish-filled lagoons, waterfalls, and two swimming pools. Reorientation of the reception, lounge, and circulation areas takes advantage of ocean and waterscape views, with new skylights providing plenty of natural light. White or pastel walls are accented by pink ceramic trim with a shell pattern in relief. Stone flooring is topped with a mix of floral and geometric patterned carpets, which define seating areas. Fully or partially upholstered chairs and sofas are awash with the rich colors of the tropics. The varied artwork throughout includes a large sculpture in one entrance lobby that depicts a school of jumping porpoises. Pillows with a shell motif, large urns filled with native flora, and other accessories enhance the decor.

Twelve individually schemed restaurants offer guests varied options of cuisine and atmosphere: hot dogs by the pool, or more formal attire while in the Cafe Martinique, for example.

Guestroom decor follows the themes introduced in the public areas. An array of soft and vibrant finishes—such as bedspreads mixing greens, reds, and blues in an overall shell pattern—emphasize the resort's Caribbean location.

ARCHITECT
WIMBERLY ALLISON TONG & GOO; THE ARCHITECTS PARTNERSHIP

INTERIOR DESIGN
WILSON & ASSOCIATES

PHOTOGRAPHY
MIKE WILSON

OPPOSITE *The registration area introduces guests to the gracious approach to relaxation found throughout Atlantis.*

ABOVE *Cavorting dolphins are represented in a focal fountain in one of the resort's lobby areas.*

In the lobby lounge, as in most of the other public areas at Atlantis, the design team embraced an oceanic theme through the use of such items as a dolphin-inspired table base.

OPPOSITE *A large tapestry depicting the flora of the island is hung in a place of honor beside a grand staircase.*

LEFT *The Seagrapes Restaurant, serving breakfast, lunch, and dinner daily, frames views through French doors of the 14-acre water park. Chair backs carved with a fish motif are a whimsical touch.*

BELOW *Guestroom options range from standard accommodations in the towers, shown, to a top-of-the-line presidential suite.*

CELEBRITY CENTURY

ABOVE *The sleek Century is the largest ship in the Celebrity fleet at a length of 815 feet.*

The 1,750-passenger Century cruise ship brings upscale elegance and sophisticated entertainment technology to the high seas aboard the largest vessel in the Celebrity fleet. Joining forces with Sony New Technologies, a division of Sony Corporation of America, Celebrity has equipped the ship with an extensive integrated entertainment system. A Broadcast Control Center features ship-to-shore satellite and teleconferencing capabilities as well as intership audio and video including motion pictures, television, computer games, and music that can be accessed through different onboard venues—via penthouse suites to interactive kiosks.

The centerpiece of the Century's live entertainment offerings is the Celebrity Theater. The 921-seat, amphitheater-style venue rises two decks high, with cantilevered balconies providing unobstructed views. The decor is themed to reflect the heavens, incorporating shooting stars and solar images along with an illuminated ceiling that creates a light show from pinpoint effects.

The aptly named Grand Restaurant is a double-tiered room with soaring bronze-finish columns rising toward a silver-leaf vaulted ceiling. The upper and lower levels—seating 472 and 574 respectively—are connected by a sweeping grand staircase, which comes to rest at the foot of a deco-inspired crystal table. Two-story cast-glass windows at the stern are adorned with a sunburst design.

Elsewhere on the ship is Images, a 140-seat bar and lounge featuring Sony

ARCHITECT
JOHN McNEECE LTD.

INTERIOR DESIGN
BIRCH COFFEY DESIGN ASSOCIATES
AM KATZOURAKIS
UNITEDESIGNERS
YATES-SILVERMAN

PHOTOGRAPHY
CELEBRITY CRUISES

ABOVE *The 921-seat Celebrity Theater is themed to reflect the moon and stars.*

LEFT *The lofty double-tiered Grand Restaurant, designed by Birch Coffey, is graced with soaring bronze columns rising toward a silver-leaf ceiling.*

ABOVE *Michael's Club, a traditional lounge and game room, evokes the ambience of a gentleman's smoking club.*

RIGHT *This luxurious onboard suite, designed by Birch Coffey as a penthouse at sea, brings a new level of sophistication to cruise accommodations.*

Playstation video tables; the 10,000-square-foot AquaSpa with a range of beauty and health treatments; Michael's Club, a 45-guest lounge styled in the tradition of a gentleman's smoking library; Tastings, a 74-seat coffee and wine bar; and the Crystal Room, a bar and lounge capturing the deco flair of classic cruise liners from the 1930s. In addition, an extensive art collection showcasing modern and contemporary works plus 91,000 square feet of open deck space make a stroll down any corridor a visual feast.

Aside from the beautifully appointed 823 standard cabins in various configurations plus 50 suites, the Century has introduced two 1,219-square-foot Penthouse Suites that can be combined with adjacent mini-suites for the ultimate luxury at sea. The contemporary, classic styling of the furnishings evokes the decor one might find in a five-star hotel suite, with added amenities here including private verandas accessible through glass doors and spacious master baths lined in marble. The Century embraces high style on the high seas, with an eye toward the next millennium.

ABOVE The 10,000-square-foot AquaSpa pampers guests with beauty treatments or leads them through active workouts; it's the passenger's call.

CARNIVAL CRUISE LINES IMAGINATION

ABOVE *The Imagination is a sleek flight of fantasy for the Carnival line.*

Imagination is an apropos name for a cruise ship that is such a flight of fantasy. Symbolizing the ship's otherworldly ambience is the gold-leafed sphinx—half woman, half lion—that is part of a series set upon tapered pilasters and overlooking the Promenade and most levels of the Grand Atrium. Each sphinx is lighted by color-changing neon, setting the stage for passengers' onboard adventures.

Other mythological creatures are used throughout the ship in various forms to express the central theme of exoticism. All elevator lobbies, for example, feature gilt goddess-faced plaques set on tapered, pink simulated-stone buttresses. Between the elevator doors are marble panels with mosaics in a classical Roman motif. Winged Mercury figures enhance the walls of the Xanadu lounge. Other public spaces may not always induce such mystical visions, but they're rich in detail and finishes nevertheless.

The Pride and Spirit restaurants are casually connected to the designer's classical theme. The Pride room features gold-leaf accents in a "V" motif, while the Spirit showcases silver-leaf "U" accents. Wall treatments in both rooms make use of polished stone panels, while brocade fabrics reinforce the luxe look. Menus are a mix of world-class cuisines.

The Dynasty Lounge is outfitted in pearwood veneers and gold and copper-colored lacquers. Hand-laid glass tile mosaics in the Venetian style are used extensively on the ceiling and furnishings. The finishing touch is a gold and sequin-adorned stage curtain with an Egyptian motif.

ARCHITECT/INTERIOR DESIGN
JOSEPH FARCUS

PHOTOGRAPHY
ANDY NEWMAN

ABOVE *The Dynasty Lounge incorporates classical
motifs in an expansive, modern space.*
LEFT *The generous pool deck aboard the
Imagination imparts a health club and spa ambience on the high seas.*

ABOVE *The various lounges aboard the Imagination live up to the ship's name. Decorated in various mystical themes, the rooms feature shiny surfaces, rich materials, and custom finishes to set the stage for adventure at sea.*

LEFT & BELOW *Architect Joe Farcus, a veteran Carnival architect, designed the ship's public spaces with fantasy in mind. Ample seating areas and glittery finishes keep passengers out of their cabins and part of the onboard festivities within the diverse lounges and cafes.*

ROYAL CARIBBEAN LEGEND OF THE SEAS

ABOVE *The Legend of the Seas is the latest in ship design, with multiple decks, balconies, and acres of glass windows and windbreaks.*

OPPOSITE *The grand staircase of the ship's multi-level atrium makes for memorable entrances evoking* Grand Hotel.

ARCHITECT
NJAL EIDE

INTERIOR DESIGN
**HOWARD SNOWEISS
DESIGN GROUP
LARS IWDAL
P.B. WILDAY
YRAN & STORBRAATEN
SMC DESIGN**

PHOTOGRAPHY
**ROYAL CARIBBEAN
CRUISE LINE**

With Royal Caribbean's newest ship, it's the berth of a legend. The 1,808-passenger Legend of the Seas was designed with two acres of windows, glass windbreaks, skylights, and window walls throughout the public spaces for an ambience of openness, water, and light. The ship also is the first to unite two of Royal Caribbean's hallmark design features: a multi-deck atrium called The Centrum and the distinctive Viking Crown Lounge. Add to that the glass-roofed Solarium—an indoor/outdoor space incorporating a swimming pool, whirlpools, seating, landscaping, and foodservice—plus an 800-seat theater, and you begin to understand the one-upmanship inherent in current cruise ship design.

Measuring 867 feet long and weighing 70,000 tons, the ship sails through the Panama Canal, on Alaskan cruises, and along the line's first-ever Hawaiian Islands treks. The top-level Sun Deck, with an outdoor swimming pool, stretches more than 118 feet from side to side and extends nearly 7 feet beyond either side of the ship's 105-foot-wide hull, making the Legend one of the widest cruise ships in the world.

Full-scale musical productions are presented in the 800-seat, amphitheater-style That's Entertainment Theater. The room spans two decks and features a wide proscenium stage and full orchestra pit. Instead of overhanging balconies, there is a trio of stepped terraces with edge-lit railings of glass imbedded with stars. The 550-seat Anchors Aweigh lounge is a smaller cabaret and nightclub serving onboard revelers.

ABOVE *The two-level Romeo and Juliet dining room features expanses of glass windows and a double staircase entry for an open, flowing feeling as guests cross toward their tables.*

Elsewhere aboard the Legend, the Spa is an expansive fitness center with exercise equipment, saunas, aerobics area, beauty salon, and massage and herbal therapy treatment rooms. The ship also features a teen center called Optix, the Club Ocean children's playroom, the V-Deck video arcade, a flexible-format conference center, casino, veranda staterooms with exterior balconies, and the two-level Romeo and Juliet dining room. Since the dining room is located in the ship's superstructure rather than the hull as on traditional ships, the room's walls are virtually all glass, framing spectacular sea views from every table.

The heraldry of international flags enhances the ambience at the window-side row of tables in the main dining room.

ABOVE & LEFT *Lounges and conversation groupings aboard the Legend exemplify the upscale furnishings program employed by the design team; it's the look of a first-rate hotel in a major international city.*

Spas &

Recreation

SCHLOSSHOTEL BÜHLERHÖHE

TOP *The hilltop site allows views across forested acres to the Rhine Valley.*

ABOVE *A cantilevered canopy marks the resort's main entrance.*

OPPOSITE *Careful restoration has returned the hotel, including the main reception lobby, to its original grace and splendor.*

ARCHITECT
ARCHITEKTENBÜRO WEIDLEPLAN

INTERIOR DESIGN
WICHERS INNENARCHITECKTUR

PHOTOGRAPHY
COURTESY OF SCHLOSSHOTEL BÜHLERHÖHE

The 90-guestroom Schlosshotel Bühlerhöhe opened in 1914 as a mountaintop retreat for Europeans and other international travelers looking to rest mind and body high above the Rhine Valley. Although the hotel is conveniently located near the famous hot baths of Baden-Baden, guests would have little reason to leave the hotel's sumptuously appointed restaurants and lounges, guestrooms, spa, and recreational facilities set on 40 private, park-like acres.

The impressive scale of the pink and gray cut-stone main building is enhanced by slate mansard roofs punctuated by white-framed windows set in dormers. Pink stucco is used for accent walls, with a series of intimate terraces and walkways linking the main structure with smaller, surrounding outbuildings.

A recent renovation and expansion program re-established the property's glorious *Grand Hotel* ambience while adding such modern features as a conference center with six meeting rooms. Foodservice options include the Imperial Restaurant, with a mix of traditional and contemporary design elements and the Schlossrestaurant, where crystal chandeliers are reflected in mirrors that ring the room.

The refurbished, classically styled spa includes an indoor pool wrapped by floor-to-ceiling windows that offer views of the valley to guests relaxing on comfortable lounge chairs or swimming. Also new is a suite of marble-accented rooms where massages, sauna, and other treatments are available to revive the spirits of guests on retreat.

ABOVE & RIGHT *New facilities include the marble-floored spa treatment area and a juice bar.*

OPPOSITE *Classically inspired statues enhance the new indoor pool area. Large windows help bring the outdoors inside during all seasons.*

ABOVE & LEFT *The Presidential Suite offers spectacular views across the Rhine Valley. Like all guestrooms, it's filled with antique and reproduction furnishings.*

OPPOSITE *A grand circular staircase with an ornamental balustrade bridges the floors in the hotel. Patterned marble flooring lends visual appeal on the main level.*

TOP & ABOVE *Contemporary lighting fixtures are bright notes in the Imperial restaurant, as are the murals by artist Wolfgang Harms.*
RIGHT *The multilevel Schlossrestaurant, with its large bay windows, presents a menu of regional specialties.*

NEW YORK, NEW YORK

STRYKERS SPORTING CLUB

TOP & ABOVE *The lobby and stairway of Strykers sport a deco look, a reference to the site's former life as a supper club in the 1930s and 40s.*

ARCHITECT/INTERIOR DESIGN
ELEVATIONS DESIGN & CONSTRUCTION CO.

PHOTOGRAPHY
PETER PAIGE

Covering 10,000 square feet on the basement level of a circa 1925 midtown Manhattan office building, the new $3-million Strykers Sporting Club provides its members with a choice of athletic activities ranging from relaxing steam rooms to more highly charged endeavors including boxing. A series of dramatically scaled and detailed spaces juxtaposes the decor associated with a traditional men's club with forms and materials that reflect the functionality of machine-oriented workouts. A strong deco influence, a reference to the site's use as a supper club in the 1930s and 40s, permeates the entire facility.

A semicircular stairway leads from street level down to the club's entrance lobby, where the strong geometric pattern created by a black-and-white terrazzo floor is gently offset by curved soffits and other architectural features. Neoclassical murals behind the reception desk key the theme of athletics. Chairs and sofas dressed in midnight blue velvet provide ample seating in the reception area.

Open to the lobby is a regulation-size 18-by-18-foot boxing ring surrounded by a sparring area, free weights, and cardiovascular equipment. From here, a vaulted terrazzo-floored corridor—its walls again decorated with murals stylistically related to those behind the reception desk—serves as the elevator lobby. Club chairs covered in black leather line one side of the space, which extends to separate locker areas for men and women, saunas, massage and whirlpool rooms, and other amenities including a barber shop and juice bar.

ABOVE & LEFT *Neoclassical murals with a deco flair enhance the walls behind the main reception desk. Chairs and sofas upholstered in midnight blue velvet provide stylish seating.*

ABOVE *The 18-by-18-foot boxing ring surrounded by a sparring area is open to the lobby.*

TOP & ABOVE *A spa and a juice bar enhance the club's amenities.*

LEFT *The main exercise area features extensive free weights and circuit machines.*

SHERATON NEW YORK HEALTH CLUB

ABOVE *Accented by video monitors set in a partition wall, the club's reception area features stainless steel, aluminum, and anigre surfaces.*

As part of a renovation assignment at this urban hotel, the design team carved a health club from an unlikely basement-level space. Conforming to the curve of the building's exterior retaining wall, the 3,500-square foot facility is essentially wedge-shaped, with a series of smaller wedges asymmetrically related to each other. The architectural and interior design schemes take advantage of the semi-circular shape, creating a radial plan with angled walls that work off the central reception area.

To allow daylight inside, the architect created an exterior wall of windows separated from the retaining wall by a 4-foot trench. Adorning the retaining wall and visible inside the gym, a 70-foot-long handpainted mural depicts a runner in a sequence of motion. Taking its color cues from the mural, the interior palette features cool blue-violet and green hues. Glass, mirrors, custom stainless steel, and brushed aluminum throughout create a light, almost transparent effect.

The reception area has been configured at an angle off the entrance, aligning itself along two circular columns clad in hand-finished aluminum. A desk is built of stainless steel and anigre wood. Eight-inch-deep blue metal fins radiate from the ceiling's center to achieve a multi-layered look. Incorporated within the columns and fins are custom light fixtures.

Functioning as a visual divider between the reception and workout areas, a partition grid of aluminum and glass has stepped openings and showcases six video monitors.

Set behind the curved reception wall are men's and women's locker rooms,

ARCHITECT
BRENNAN BEER GORMAN/ARCHITECTS

INTERIOR DESIGN
BRENNAN BEER GORMAN MONK/INTERIORS

PHOTOGRAPHY
PETER PAIGE

again employing stainless steel and mirrored surfaces. White tiles flecked with blue and green accent the overall color scheme. Custom millwork lockers complement stainless steel countertops surrounding cantilevered, white porcelain sinks. Custom lighting fixtures echo the motif of the column covers. Each locker room has two showers, a private steam room, and a sauna.

EQUINOX FITNESS CLUB

A full-service health club, the upscale Manhattan facility is designed to attract young working professionals via areas dedicated to cardiovascular fitness, massage therapy, sports psychology, nutrition, and other specialties. Housed in a historic building in the Flatiron district that was a department store at the turn-of-the-century, the two-floor gym contrasts high-tech, industrial elements with the backdrop of classical cast-iron columns and rail details. "The fact that it was a landmark building set up a lot of parameters that we had to follow, but also helped us pick a direction and philosophy for the design," according to the designer. "The new intervention, which is manifestly different from the character of the original space, emphatically asserts itself while relying on the abstracted quality of the original space to create a dialogue between old and new."

ABOVE *A health food cafe and colorful reception desk greet Equinox members at the club's entrance.*
OPPOSITE *New steel and glass divider walls are juxaposed with existing cast-iron columns.*

ARCHITECT/INTERIOR DESIGN
MOJO STUMER ASSOCIATES

PHOTOGRAPHY
FRANK ZIMMERMAN

Arriving visitors are greeted with a retail sports shop to the right and a health food cafe on the left. The main reception desk is a composition of projecting planes in steel and colorful laminates. Slate flooring paves the main circulation route, with a newly added metal staircase connecting upper and lower levels and the expanded mezzanine. Throughout, canopies of metal-framed, textured glass affixed to the gracious columns define transition areas between public and private zones. Other predominant materials used to underscore the clarity of the design intent include copper, zinc, precast concrete panels, and recycled rubber flooring.

ABOVE *A newly inserted staircase connects the levels of the fitness club.*

RIGHT *The retail shop rests to the right of the main entrance.*

FAR RIGHT *The former turn-of-the-century department store has found new life as a high style "sweat shop."*

THE FISHER ISLAND CLUB

ABOVE *The Mediterranean design influences, including stucco walls and tile roofing, of original buildings on the Vanderbilt estate were adapted for new facilities.*

ARCHITECT
SANDY & BABCOCK, INC.

INTERIOR DESIGN
CAROLE KORN INTERIORS, INC.

PHOTOGRAPHY
**PAUL BARTON
STEVEN BROOKE
MARK SURLOFF
JOHN GILLAN**

The Fisher Island Club is an exclusive resort contained within a larger residential community off the coast of Miami, Florida. The entire resort takes its stylistic direction from the original resort enclave built in the 1920s by William K. Vanderbilt, and many of the Club's facilities are housed in restored portions of the estate. Club accommodations include 60 guestrooms and suites distributed among the former crew quarters, four restored cottages, and new villas. Restaurants, night club, lounges, spa, tennis courts, golf course, and swimming pools complete the amenities.

Buildings are finished in hand-troweled stucco and complemented by cast-stone columns and archways. Hand-painted decorative tiles are used as accents, and hand-made, terra-cotta roof tiles—manufactured by the same firm that created the original ones for the estate—lend a historically correct touch.

The Mediterranean-style Spa Internazionale, created within the cavernous space of a now fully redesigned airplane hangar, covers 22,000 square feet and offers European and American health treatments. VIP suites are available on a full- and part-day basis and provide a private steam bath, sauna, whirlpool spa, massage table, shower, aerobic studio, and lounge area. Others can take advantage of exfoliation treatments, body wraps, aromatherapy, and facial services.

More active spa attendees can enjoy an indoor lap pool with a retractable roof, an outdoor pool, a whirlpool bath with cold-plunge, or take advantage of personal trainers and a selection of exercise machines.

ABOVE *The Spa Internazionale was fashioned from an airplane hangar used by the original owners*

LEFT *Buildings are arranged across the grounds to take advantage of beach and water views.*

RIGHT *Guestroom terraces provide a private place to dine or take advantage of a whirlpool spa.*

BELOW *Boutique-style guestroom accommodations include converted cottages and new villas offering comfortable, contemporary interiors.*

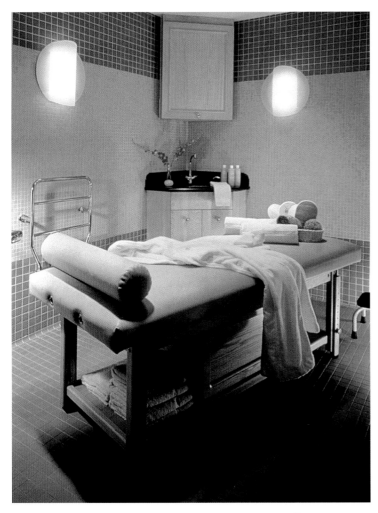

ABOVE LEFT *Treatment and massage rooms in the Spa Internazionale are appointed with the same level of style as other areas in the facility.*

ABOVE RIGHT *The grandly scaled architectural features found within the original buildings at the Fisher Island Club were restored to Vanderbilt-era grandeur.*

LEFT *Seven different venues at the Club, including this cabaret space, offer a range of gourmet dining and entertainment options.*

The Sportin

HILTON HEAD ISLAND, SOUTH CAROLINA
COLLETON RIVER PLANTATION

From its inception, the Colleton River Plantation was inspired by the graceful beauty of traditional buildings in the South Carolina low country. The club's 700-acre site—with a golf course designed by Jack Nicklaus and room for 395 home sites—is bordered by a 1,200-acre state nature preserve and provides residents access to the Atlantic Ocean via the Intercoastal Waterway.

The 32,000-square-foot clubhouse successfully combines features such as handcrafted, wood-molded bricks, slate roofing, shutters, and columned verandas. Inside, the large space is broken down into a series of wings and pavilions. The pool house, tennis facilities, and other multi-use cottages dot the property as in original plantation outbuilding arrangements.

The main floor includes a member's dining room with focal fireplace, a private dining room, mixed grill, and lounge that all radiate from a central lobby. Furnishings reflect the building's exterior style. A hand-made, custom-designed area rug in the lobby/reception area is based on an antique Serape design. Carefully selected antique seating and casegoods add character to each room. Crystal, brass, and verde chandeliers are suspended from high ceilings trimmed with decorative moldings.

While the richly colored and textured fabrics, wallcoverings, and floorcoverings work hand-in-hand to impart a high level of elegance to the club, the overall ambience is warm, welcoming, and reminiscent of a comfortable private residence in the genteel South.

ARCHITECT
NICHOLS CARTER & GRANT ARCHITECTS

INTERIOR DESIGN
MARCIA DAVIS & ASSOCIATES, INC.

PHOTOGRAPHY
GABRIEL BENZUR

ABOVE *Club members may take advantage of full-service dining facilities and comfortable lounge areas.*

ABOVE LEFT *The pro shop is outfitted in a design style complementary to the club's other interiors.*
LEFT *Plantation shutters are an appropriately regional method to control sunlight in many of the club's public spaces.*

LAS MISIONES CLUB CAMPESTRE

ABOVE *Spanish Colonial architecture was the inspiration for the design of the club, the entrance facade of which is shown here.*

OPPOSITE *An overscaled domed reception lobby is the main circulation hub for the club.*

ARCHITECT
ADOLFO SAVIGNON
SONIA V. DE SANTOS

INTERIOR DESIGN
JAMES NORTHCUTT
ASSOCIATES

PHOTOGRAPHY
JAIME ARDILES-ARCE

The team involved with the design of Las Misiones Club Campestre has achieved the seemingly paradoxical combination of grandly scaled opulence and comfort. Set in the foothills between two mountain ranges, the main building presents soaring rooflines, a domed entrance, bell tower, and other features that recall an ancient Spanish Colonial cloister.

Columns, capitals, portals, and additional architectural details fashioned from local gray Cantera stone were created by carvers who worked on site for more than two years. Such painstaking attention is also evidenced inside, where local granite is used for paving and other flooring combining a flamed finish with polished inlays. Walls throughout the clubhouse are finished with a glazed and distressed plaster coating, an intriguing yet unobtrusive backdrop for fine furnishings.

The club is entered through a rotunda topped by a 30-foot-diameter brick dome, from which members and guests proceed directly to the main dining room. A 20-foot-high ceiling, supported by rough-hewn wood beams, creates a nave-like effect. Floor-to-ceiling windows on two sides of the room provide views of the mountainscape. Custom rugs rich in earthy colors— charcoal, terra cotta, cream, and magenta— anchor lounge seating pieces covered with chenilles and silks. Stone and wood are mixed for focal tables, while dining tables are topped with polished granite. Dining chairs are made of woven raffia for a decidedly Spanish touch. Other amenities include a "19th Hole" restaurant, private dining rooms, and an outdoor terrace. On the level below are locker rooms, the pro shop, and direct access to the links.

LEFT & BELOW *Outdoor dining allows club members to take advantage of views across the landscape, while trelliswork and market umbrellas help keep things cool.*

BOTTOM *A series of arcades opens into the timber-ceilinged main dining room.*

SPANISH HILLS
GOLF & COUNTRY CLUB

Designed as the centerpiece of a 420-acre residential development less than an hour north of Los Angeles, the 36,637-square-foot clubhouse sits on a knoll to give virtually every room a view of the mountains or the Pacific. Reflecting the region's heritage of Spanish Colonial mansions and ranchos built in the 1920s and 1930s, the building's architectural design features arches, courtyards, fountains, terraces, towers, a red tile roof, and intricate detailing of mosaic tile and carved stone.

The plan places dining and lounge areas around the building perimeter, with a large kitchen and administrative offices at the core. The covered north entrance opens to the men's lounge and locker area on the west and the club grill on the east, in turn leading to the main dining spaces. The men's lounge features three large windows capped with fanlights, a cherry-stained wood bar, and furnishings upholstered in a plum-colored fabric. In the main lounge the palette is softer, with millwork, walls, and other structural elements finished in neutral tones to coordinate with fabrics and carpeting. Dark-stained casegoods and doors, an iron chandelier, and an idyllic mural complete the space.

An arcade screens off the lounge from the main dining room, where a curved window wall and French doors provide a connection to the outdoors. Columns and ceiling coffers define seating areas in the room, which can accommodate up to 140. Crystal drops give the wrought-iron chandeliers

ABOVE *The curved wall of the dining room is pierced by large windows to let in natural light. An adjoining terrace services dining, cocktails, and other gatherings.*
OPPOSITE *A decorative chandelier is a focal point in the club's entrance vestibule.*

ARCHITECT/INTERIOR DESIGN
ALTEVERS ASSOCIATES
PHOTOGRAPHY
MILROY/MCALEER

added brilliance above chairs upholstered in a floral fabric. A private dining room, created through movable dividers, and adjacent terrace dining is also available. The pool area is located away from the terrace to make way for a broad lawn where special event tents may also be raised.

The sloping site of the clubhouse leaves plenty of space at the rear elevation for additional amenities below the main function level. Directly below the men's lounge is a women's locker room and 30-seat lounge featuring stained ash detailing. Adjacent is a fully equipped fitness center for men and women, an employee lounge, and a pro shop.

ABOVE *The main lounge is a comfortable place to meet before dinner in the adjacent main dining room.*

LEFT *Stained millwork, including that used for the coffered ceiling and the bar, add an appropriately masculine feeling to the men's lounge at Spanish Hills.*

OPPOSITE *A total of 140 can be seated in the main dining room below a series of chandeliers with elegant crystal drops.*

WAILEA GOLD & EMERALD CLUBHOUSE

ABOVE *The new clubhouse services two adjacent golf courses as part of the larger Wailea Resort.*
OPPOSITE *The clubhouse's architecture showcases the vernacular Hawaiian plantation style.*

ARCHITECT
WIMBERLY ALLISON TONG & GOO

INTERIOR DESIGN
DESIGN MASTERS, INC.

PHOTOGRAPHY
KYLE ROTHENBERG

The Wailea Gold and Emerald Clubhouse is part of the Wailea Golf Club complex, which encompasses three 18-hole golf courses, two clubhouses, maintenance facilities, and a training facility within the 1,500-acre Wailea Resort. The stand-alone clubhouse is flanked by two championship golf courses designed by Robert Trent Jones II, and is within a five-minute drive of the resort's five beachfront resort hotels, six condominium complexes, and six single-family residential communities. Catering to an upscale market of affluent tourists and resort residents, the low, Hawaiian plantation estate-style structure showcases elements of the region's architecture with intricate, ceramic-tile roof lines, limestone columns, stucco exterior walls, wide overhangs, vine-covered pergolas, French doors, lanais, whitewashed oak finishes, and moss rock walls. The complex also incorporates two soothing water features, an elegant porte cochere, expansive lobby with atrium, and men's and women's lounges.

The design minimizes walls in order to showcase spectacular views of the ocean, the offshore islands of Kahoolawe and Molokini, Mount Haleakala, and golf course fairways. The clubhouse restaurant—with vaulted ceiling, 10-foot-high doors, and granite flooring—offers more than 9,500 feet of dining space, about half of which is upon scenic terraces. Meanwhile, the landscaping plan emphasizes indigenous plants such as bromeliads, hala, ilima, lauae fern, and coconuts. Lots of comfortable, informal space is created by lattice-covered lanais and terraces, skylights, and interior landscaping that help to blur the

ABOVE Breakfasting on the landscaped lanai is a golfer's paradise at the Wailea Gold & Emerald.

boundaries between indoors and out.

A large full-service pro shop with extensive retail space shares the main level with the porte cochere, entryway, lobby, formal lounges, restaurant, kitchen, offices, and locker rooms. Car service and storage areas are nestled unobtrusively on the lower level of the sloping site. ADA solutions include pedestrian access to public areas and lower service areas via an elevator, braille on all signage, and accessible telephones and bathroom facilities.

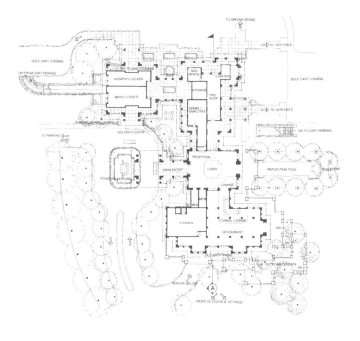

ABOVE *The furnishings here and throughout the club are casual, in keeping with classic Hawaiian island living.*

RIGHT *A generously sized pro shop is a member and guest crowd-pleaser at the club.*

PUERTO VALLARTA, MEXICO

HOTEL BEL-AIR PUERTO VALLARTA

Successful resorts located in warm-weather climates must offer a balance between outdoor recreational areas where guests can revel in the sunshine and interior spaces where they can relax in cool comfort away from the midday heat. Such a balance has been well achieved at the recently renovated and expanded Hotel Bel-Air Puerto Vallarta.

The centerpiece of the 10-acre resort is a building whose exterior exudes Spanish style. Red tile roofs delineate the staggered heights of the structure, which is clad with pink-tinged stucco punctuated by arcades and the arched openings of windows and doors. Just inside the canopied entrance is a reception lobby with 20-foot ceilings. At the center of the lobby, a fountain decorated with colorful Mexican ceramic tiles serves as a visual and aural focal point. Lush interior plantscaping heightens the oasis-like ambience. Just off the lobby are conference rooms that can be broken out to serve groups of up to 80. Nearby is a newly built fitness and health pavilion.

The resort's main dining room, called Il Candil, seats 60 on three levels. The attractive room features pale pink walls capped by a domed ceiling. Ornately hand-carved wood chairs have rush seats topped by colorfully patterned cushions. Tall double doors ring one side of the room and offer easy access to a patio, where guests often congregate for breakfast and lunch. Just steps from

ARCHITECT/INTERIOR DESIGN
PLAN ARQUITECTOS

PHOTOGRAPHY
MILROY/MCALEER

ABOVE *A swimming pool with brilliantly colored blue mosaic tile accents is a popular relaxation spot beside the main hotel building.*

OPPOSITE *Evening hours are ideal for alfresco dining.*

the dining room and adjacent to the new fitness pavilion, a circular pool is trimmed with blue mosaic tiles. Market umbrellas and private cabanas draped with crisp white fabric offer shade from the sun.

All guestrooms—42 in the main building and 25 villas with one-, two-, or three-bedrooms—have walls painted in various pastels; there are five separate color combinations throughout the 67 units. Private terraces with whirlpool spas and marble-clad bathrooms are standard, while each villa is enhanced by a kitchenette and outdoor plunge pool.

ABOVE *Seating in the domed dining room is set on tiers to provide each guest with views of the lushly landscaped grounds.*

RIGHT *Guestrooms are generously proportioned and include tile floors and brightly hued fabrics.*

PALACE OF THE LOST CITY

ABOVE *Fantastic architectural creations surround the close to 17 acres of water features. Even the lifeguard stations carry out the design concept.*
OPPOSITE *The golf clubhouse was constructed with a blend of natural rock formations and precast concrete elements.*

ARCHITECT
WIMBERLY ALLISON TONG & GOO
ASSOCIATED ARCHITECT
BURG DOHERTY BRYANT & PARTNERS
INTERIOR DESIGN
WILSON & ASSOCIATES

PHOTOGRAPHY
DAVE LINDSAY
RON MITCHELL

An empty 80-acre site about 100 miles northwest of Johannesburg, South Africa, has been transformed into a 350-guestroom destination resort. An entertainment center with casino, two golf courses and clubhouse, extensive water features, and landscaped grounds offers virtually every amenity for the active or leisure-oriented visitor.

The design of the resort was cued by a legend devised by the design team in which a king's palatial realm is rediscovered after untold centuries. "Unearthed" was a massive main palace, rising from one to eight stories, with soaring towers topped by domes seemingly constructed of elephant tusks and palm fronds from which spring cranes, monkeys, and other African animals. These decorative elements are among more than 15,000 precast concrete features created for the site.

The entrance to the hotel is along an axis that leads from a bridge to an 87-foot-high lobby with a mural of regional flora and fauna capping the space. Floors of intricately patterned marble complement large planters anchoring full-height replicated palm trees. Beyond this space is the Crystal Court terrace, where dining is amid columns with elephant foot-based columns. Additional pavilions, courtyards, and lounges abound. The opulent architecture is complemented by locally made furnishings including seating and casegoods, fabrics, artwork, and accessories. Also on site are a golf clubhouse and other easlily accessible sporting facilities.

The design team was equally creative with the theme in the 330 guestrooms and 21 suites. Animal and plant motifs are used for fabrics and carpets, carved into wooden furniture, and also found on lamp bases.

OPPOSITE *The solidity of the clubhouse structure is echoed inside, as in this lounge and dining area.*

LEFT AND BELOW *Clubhouse terraces provide ideal perches from which to follow play on the two on-site 18-hole championship golf courses designed by Gary Player.*

FOUR SEASONS RESORT AVIARA GOLF CLUBHOUSE

The clubhouse at the Four Seasons Resort Aviara is the initial, central element of a 1,000-acre, master-planned community that will eventually include a five-star, 350-room hotel with a sport center. The resort is located at the banks of Batiquitos Lagoon—a rich habitat for wetland birds and plants—amid the rolling hills and valleys of the southern California coast. The 30,000-square-foot, two-story clubhouse evokes the Spanish colonial architecture of early California; its clay tile roofs, exposed wood eaves, and plaster-clad exterior evoke an elegant regional flavor that remains casual enough for a resort setting. The clubhouse was designed to set the tone architecturally for the hotel and private houses which will be developed nearby.

Set into the sloping hillside site, the Aviara clubhouse presents a low-key one-story facade to the street and along view corridors toward neighboring homes. Rooflines are kept simple, with extensive landscaping and berms screening the building so that guests can enjoy the natural, residential setting.

Outfitted with rich materials including marble, stone, stucco, and dark-stained millwork, the club's interiors are appointed with comfortable furnishings that evoke the ambience of a classic early-century California villa. Overstuffed sofas and chairs blend with leather upholstered pieces, tapestry fabrics, and antique-finished lamps and accessories.

The club's amenities include a restaurant, bar, lounge, locker rooms, pro shop, snack bar, golf academy, and 10,000-square-foot maintenance facility.

ABOVE With views across the manicured golf course, the two-story Aviara clubhouse evokes the Spanish Colonial architecture of early California. OPPOSITE Guests may dine or converse beneath market umbrellas on the clubhouse's south terrace overlooking the lush grounds.

ARCHITECT/INTERIOR DESIGN
WIMBERLY ALLISON TONG & GOO

INTERIOR DESIGN
WILSON & ASSOCIATES

PHOTOGRAPHY
DAVE LINDSAY

ABOVE *An interior fountain graces the entrance lobby, which is finished in attractive textural materials including stone, marble, and stucco.*

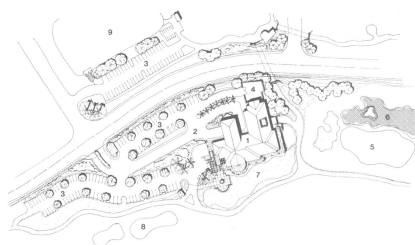

LEFT & BELOW *The look of an early-century California villa keys the decor of the club, with overstuffed sofas, tapestry fabrics, and antique-finish accessories.*

BROKEN TOP GOLF CLUBHOUSE

ABOVE *Stone, wood, glass, and metal were used to tie the clubhouse to the surrounding environment.* **OPPOSITE** *In the great room, a massive stone fireplace takes center stage.*

ARCHITECT
WIMBERLY ALLISON TONG & GOO

INTERIOR DESIGN
RCI, INC.

PHOTOGRAPHY
LAURIE BLACK
DICK BUSHER

This new clubhouse is the focal point for the 500-acre Broken Top residential/resort community. Servicing a championship golf course designed by Tom Weiskopf and Jay Morrish, the club does double duty as a winter retreat for skiers who frequent nearby Mt. Bachelor. Evoking the prairie style of architectural icon Frank Lloyd Wright, the building also echoes the rugged elegance of the environment, filled with boulders, rocky ledges, brush, and the volcanic peaks of the neighboring Cascade Mountains. The site is a plateau set 15 feet above the surrounding landscape, affording 360-degree views.

Two massive sandstone walls, locally quarried and cut, are the linchpins of the club's design. Unbroken in line from ground level to roof, the walls coincide with Earth's cardinal points, one laid north to south, the other east to west. The four quadrants defined by the two walls are the structure around which a framework of cedar trusses, expanses of glass, and a copper roof revolves. The framework is carefully crafted and assembled with concealed connections and recessed bolting. Four predominant materials—stone, wood, glass, and copper—relate the structure to the natural world.

The approach to the clubhouse is from a gently rising road leading to a porte cochere. From the entry foyer, which features hand-carved doors, patrons enter the great room, where exposed cedar trusses support the copper roof. A massive, freestanding stone fireplace towers out of a base of natural boulders. Leather sofas, clean-lined wood tables and chairs, and Indian motif fabrics allow the architecture to dominate. An adjoining terrace encourages outdoor functions and dining during warmer seasons. Also on this main level are two dining rooms and a members' grill, which all frame vistas of the mountains and lake.

A grand staircase, created from huge natural boulders, joins the entry level to lower function areas. Cedar stairs descend over and through the boulders to the lower level, where a pro shop, locker rooms, exercise area, swimming complex, conference room, storage and repair facilities, and service yard orchestrate a golfer's haven.

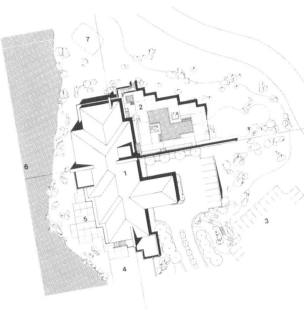

ABOVE *Tall window walls provide almost unobstructed views to the golf course.*

LEFT *Boulders serve as decorative elements along the club's grand staircase.*

OPPOSITE *Materials and building methods were left unmasked throughout the interiors.*

RIGHT *Members can choose from among two dining rooms and a lounge in which to take meals and refreshments.*

BELOW *A terrace adjoining a dining room is cantilevered over the rocky banks of the lake.*

OPPOSITE *A passageway cut through the stone wall of a terrace frames a distant view.*

METEDECONK NATIONAL GOLF CLUB

ABOVE The design team created an unassuming exterior for a new guestroom and entertainment facility, which blends well with the forested site.
OPPOSITE High ceilings and large windows bring sunlight into the multipurpose public areas.

ARCHITECT/INTERIOR DESIGN
SHELTON, MINDEL & ASSOCIATES

PHOTOGRAPHY
DAN CORNISH

The Metedeconk National Golf Club recently added the Trent Jones Cottage to host a select number of overnight guests and to service business- and entertainment-related occasions. Tucked within a stand of trees at the center of the golf course, the cottage has an unpretentious, residential appearance. Its 2,500 square feet of space is defined by a darkly stained wood exterior that is gabled and rises two stories.

The main entrance to the cottage is via a porch into a vestibule. From here, a corridor leading to the right accesses a guestroom (upstairs are three more). Straight ahead from the vestibule, a double-height stair hall (and an entrance to a kitchen) opens into a great room combining living and dining functions. Large windows frame the landscape and provide natural light, reflected off the white walls and ceiling. Neutral carpets cover portions of the wood floor.

The living room is graced with a sofa and lounge chairs covered in solid and patterned fabrics offering bright spots of color. A console visually divides this space from the dining area, where wood chairs are set around a modular dining table. Here one wall has built-in storage space including a serving counter and wet bar. The great room was planned for flexibility, with tables and seating pieces easily rearranged to meet immediate requirements.

The bedrooms carry out an aesthetic echoing that of the communal areas. In each room a white chair rail divides a unique pair of pale paint colors set off by neutral-toned carpet and bed covers. Chairs, minimal accessories, and clean-lined casegoods complete the scheme.

OPPOSITE *A mix of old- and new-style furniture sets a classic tone.*
ABOVE LEFT *Tables and chairs are easily rearranged to accommodate business and social functions.*
LEFT & ABOVE RIGHT *Furnishings in the guestrooms provide a stylish residential appeal.*

Directory

PROPERTIES

Atlantis
Paradise Island
P. O. Box N4-777
Nassau
Bahamas
Tel: (809) 363-2202
Fax: (809) 363-3703

Bora Bora Lagoon Resort
Motu Toopua, B.P. 175, Vaitape
Bora Bora
French Polynesia
Tel: 689/60-40-00
Fax: 689/60-40-01

Brasstown Valley
6321 US Highway 76
Young Harris, Georgia 30582
Tel: (706) 379-9999
Fax: (706) 379-9900

Broken Top Golf Clubhouse
61999 Broken Top Drive
Bend, Oregon 97702
Tel: (503) 383-7600

Celebrity Century
Celebrity Cruises
5201 Blue Lagoon Drive
Miami, Florida 33126
Tel: (305) 599-2600

Cobblers Cove
Godoing Bay, Speightstown
Barbados
Tel: (809) 422-2291
Fax: (809) 422-1460

Colleton River Plantation
P. O. Box 22989
Hilton Head Island, South Carolina 29925
Tel: (803) 837-3030
Fax: (803) 837-6540

Disney's Wilderness Lodge
Walt Disney World
4510 North Fort Wilderness Trail
Lake Buena Vista, Florida 32830
Tel: (407) 824-2900
Fax: (407) 824-3508

El Conquistador
Resort & Country CLub
Highway 3, Km 51.4
Las Croabas, Fajardo, 00738
Puerto Rico
Tel: (809) 860-1000
Fax: (809) 253-0178

Equinox Fitness Club
897 Broadway
New York, New York 10003
Tel: (212) 780-9300
Fax: (212) 780-9760

The Fisher Island Club
One Fisher Island Drive
Fisher Island, Florida 33109
Tel: (305) 535-6026
Fax: (305) 535-6037

Four Seasons Resort Aviara
Golf Clubhouse
7447 Batiquitos Drive
Carlsbad, California 92009
Tel: (619) 929-0077

Four Seasons Resort Nevis
P.O. Box 565
Pinneys Beach
Nevis
West Indies
Tel/Fax: (809) 469-1111

Hotel Bel-Air Costa Careyes
KM 5B Carretera Manzanillo
Puerto Vallarta
La Huerta 48970
Mexico

Hotel Bel-Air Puerto Vallarta
Pelicanos 311 Marina Vallarta
Puerto Vallarta, 48354
Mexico
Tel: (52) 322-10800
Fax: (52) 322-10801

Hyatt Regency Coolum
International Resort & Spa
P. O. Box 78
Coolum Beach, Queensland 4573
Australia
Tel: (074) 46 1234
Fax: (074) 46 2957

Imagination
Carnival Cruise Lines
3655 NW 87th Avenue
Miami, Florida 33178
Tel: (305) 599-2600
Fax: (305) 599-8630

Jean-Michel Cousteau Fiji Islands Resort
c/o Post Office
Savusavu
Fiji Islands
Tel: 679-850-188
Fax: 679-850-340

Las Misiones Club Campestre
Lazaro Cardenas 2475
Desp. "F"
66260 Garza Garcia, N.L.
Monterrey
Mexico
Tel: (52) 83-63-10-25
Fax: (52) 83-63-15-34

Legend of the Seas
Royal Caribbean Cruise Line
150 Caribbean Way
Miami, Florida 33132
Tel: (305) 539-6573
Fax: (305) 539-0140

Le Touessrok Hotel and Il-Aux-Cerfs
Trou d'Eau Douce
Flacq
Mauritius

The Little Nell
675 East Durant Avenue
Aspen, Colorado 81611
Tel: (970) 920-4600
Fax: (970) 920-4670

Lodge at Koele
The Lana'i Company, Inc.
650 Iwilei Road, Suite 202
Honolulu, Hawaii 96817
Tel: (808) 545-3913
Fax: (808) 545-7917

Londolozi Game Reserve
P.O. Box 1211
Sunninghill 2157
South Africa
Tel: 11 8038421
Fax: 11 8031810

The Mayflower Inn
118 Woodbury Road
Washington, Connecticut 06793
Tel: (860) 868-9466
Fax: (860) 868-1497

Metedeconk National Golf Club
Hannah Hill Road
Jackson, New Jersey 08527
Tel: (908) 370-7007
Fax: (908) 928-4639

Mowana Safari Lodge
P.O. Box 266
Kasane
Botswana
Tel: (276) 650300
Fax: (267) 650301

Nusa Dua Beach Hotel
P.O. Box 1028
Denpasar, Bali
Indonesia
Tel: (361) 771210
Fax: (361) 771-229

Palace of The Lost City
P.O. Box 308
Sun City 0316
South Africa
Tel: 27-1465-73000
Fax: 27-1465-73111

The Peaks at Telluride
136 Country Club Drive
P. O. Box 2702
Telluride, Colorado 81435
Tel: (970) 728-6800
Fax: (970) 728-6175

Post Ranch Inn
P. O. Box 219, Highway 1
Big Sur, California 93920
Tel: (408) 667-2200
Fax: (408) 667-2824

Schlosshotel Bühlerhöhe
Schwarzwaldhochstrasse 1
D-77815 Bühl/Baden-Baden
Germany
Tel: (0 72 26) 55-0
Fax: (0 72 26) 55-777

Sheraton Inn at Timika
P.O. Box 3
Timika 98663
Irian Jaya Island
Indonesia
Tel: 62-979-549-4949
Fax: 62-979-549-4950

Sheraton New York Health Club
Sheraton New York Hotel
811 Seventh Avenue
New York, New York 10019
Tel: (212) 841-6500
Fax: (212) 841-6504

Spanish Hills Golf & Country Club
999 Crestive Avenue
Camarillo, California 93010
Tel: (805) 388-5000

Strykers Sporting Club
167 West 46th Street
New York, New York 10036
Tel: (212) 944-1600
Fax: (212) 719-1614

Wailea Gold & Emerald Clubhouse
100 Wailea Golf Club Drive
Wailea, Maui, Hawaii 96753
Tel: (808) 875-5111

Wyoming Inn
P.O. Box 30505
Jackson, Wyoming 83001
Tel: (307) 734-0035
Fax: (307) 734-0037

ARCHITECTS & DESIGNERS

Altevers Associates
8910 University Center Lane, #250
San Diego, California 92122
Tel: (619) 535-9777
Fax: (619) 535-1181

Architects Van Lom Edwards, AIA, PC
34 NW First, Suite 309
Portland, Oregon 97209
Tel: (503) 226-0590
Fax: (503) 273-8649

Birch Coffey Design Associates
206 East 63rd Street, Suite 3
New York, New York 10021
Tel: (212) 371-0100
Fax: (212) 371-0104

Brennan Beer Gorman/Architects
Brennan Beer Gorman Monk/Interiors
515 Madison Avenue
New York, New York 10022
Tel: (212) 888-7663
Fax: (212) 888-3863

Carole Korn Interiors, Inc.
622 Banyan Trail
Boca Raton, Florida 33431
Tel: (407) 997-2888
Fax: (407) 997-2297

Cooper Carry Architects
3520 Piedmont Road, NE
Atlanta, Georgia 30305
Tel: (404) 237-2000
Fax: (404) 237-0276

Elevations Design &
Construction Company
1560 Broadway, Suite 7099
New York, New York 10036
Tel: (212) 719-1620
Fax: (212) 719-1614

Janet Freed
Jean-Michel Cousteau Fiji Islands Resort
400 Pacific Avenue, 2nd Floor West
San Francisco, California 94133
Tel: (415) 788-5796
Fax: (415) 788-0150

Joseph Farcus
5285 Pine Tree Drive
Miami Beach, Florida 33140
Tel: (305) 866-0818
Fax: (305) 866-3660

Gomez Associates
506-504 East 74 Street
New York, New York 10021
Tel: (212) 288-6829
Fax: (212) 288-1590

Hagman Yaw Architects
0123 Emma Road, Suite 200
Basalt, Colorado 81621
Tel: (970) 927-3822

Hellmuth, Obata & Kassabaum, Inc.
One Metropolitan Square
211 North Broadway, Suite 600
St. Louis, Missouri 63102
Tel: (314) 421-2000
Fax: (314) 421-6073

Hirsch/Bedner Associates
3216 Nebraska Avenue
Santa Monica, California 90404
Tel: (310) 829-9087

Howard Snoweiss Design Group
4200 Aurora Street
Coral Gables, Florida 33146
Tel: (305) 858-4114
Fax: (310) 659-7120

James Northcutt Associates
717 North La Cienega Boulevard
Los Angeles, California 90069
Tel: (310) 659-8595
Fax: (310) 659-7120

John McNeece Ltd.
2 Holford Yard
Cruikshank Street
London WCIX 9HD
United Kingdom
Tel: (44) 71-837-1225
Fax: (44) 71-837-1233

Joszi Meskan Associates
479 Ninth Street
San Francisco, California
Tel: (415) 431-0500
Fax: (415) 431-9339

Marcia Davis & Associates, Inc.
4090 Wieuca Road, NE
Atlanta, Georgia 30342
Tel: (404) 255-5600
Fax: (404) 255-1555

Mojo Stumer Associates
55 Bryant Avenue
Roslyn, New York 11576
Tel: (516) 625-3344
Fax: (516) 625-3428

Nichols Carter Grant Architects, Inc.
One Baltimore Place, Suite 401
Atlanta, Georgia 30308
Tel: (404) 892-44510
Fax: (404) 892-6424

Plan Arquitectos
Loma Bonita 7
11950 DF
Mexico
Tel: (525) 257-0097
Fax: (525) 257-1447

Luke Polder
Africa International
Design and Project Services
P. O. Box 40542
Gaborone
Botswana
Tel: (267) 372758

Profurn Contracts
P.O. Box 45, Ferndale
Randburg 2160
South Africa

Sandy & Babcock, Inc.
2727 SW 26th Avenue
Miami, Florida 33133
Tel: (305) 856-2021
Fax: (305) 856-0854

Arnold Savran, AIA
The Lanai Company, Inc.
10900 Wilshire Boulevard, Suite 610
Los Angeles, California 91132
Tel: (310) 208-8845
Fax: (310) 208-1132

Shelton, Mindel & Associates
216 West 18th Street
New York, New York 10011
Tel: (212) 243-3939
Fax: (212) 727-7310

Yates-Silverman
4045 South Industrial Road
Las Vegas, Nevada 89103
Tel: (702) 791-5606

Thorne & Cleaves
27 Apple Lane
Roxbury, Connecticut 06776
Tel: (860) 350-6185

Wilson & Associates
3811 Turtle Creek Boulevard, 15th Floor
Dallas, Texas 75219-4419
Tel: (214) 521-6753
Fax: (214) 521-0207

Wilson & Associates
8342½ Melrose Avenue
Los Angeles, California 90069
Tel: (213) 651-3234
Fax: (213) 852-4758

Wimberly Allison Tong & Goo
2222 Kalakaua Avenue, Penthouse
Honolulu, Hawaii 96815
Tel: (808) 922-1253
Fax: (808) 931-1692

Wimberly Allison Tong & Goo
140 Newport Center Drive, Suite 200
Newport Beach, California 92660
Tel: (714) 759-8923
Fax: (714) 759-3473

PHOTOGRAPHERS

Jaime Ardiles-Arce
730 Fifth Avenue
New York, New York 10019
Tel: (212) 686-4220

Paul Barton
101 West 18th Street
New York, New York 10011
Tel: (212) 533-1422

Benzur Architectural Photography, Inc.
1989 Continental Drive, NE
Atlanta, Georgia 30345
Tel: (404) 634-7259

Berger/Conser
2118 Wilshire Boulevard #752
Santa Monica, California 90403
Tel: (310) 822-8258

Steven Brooke
7910 SW 54 Court
Miami, Florida 33143
Tel: (305) 667-8075

Conservation Corporation
P.O. Box 1211
Sunninghill 2157
South Africa
Tel: 11 8038421
Fax: 11 8031810

Dan Cornish
38 Evergreen Road
New Canaan, Connecticut 06842
Tel: (203) 972-3714

Dave Marlow Photography
Aspen Skiing Company
P.O. Box 1248
Aspen, Colorado 81612
Tel: (970) 544-3072

Heidi A. Davis
Riddell Photographics
P. O. Box 2962
Jackson, Wyoming 83001
Tel: (307) 733-5353
Fax: (307) 733-5321

Jack Drafahl
Image Concepts
1187 NE 257 H Avenue
Hillsboro, Oregon 97124
Tel: (503) 648-3311
Fax: (503) 640-5397

John Gillan
14378 SW 97th Lane
Miami, Florida 33186
Tel: (305) 251-4784

Larry Dale Gordon
Coastlands
Big Sur, California 93920
Tel: (408) 667-2300

Jeffrey Asher Photography
Lana'i Company, Inc.
P. O. Box 310
Lana'i City, Hawaii 96763
Tel: (808) 565-3924
Fax: (808) 565-3881

Joe Stewardson Photography
903 Glen Arden Way, NE
Atlanta, Georgia 30306
Tel: (404) 875-4239

John Kane
Silver Sun Studios
45 West Street Commons, 1st Floor
New Milford, Connecticut 06776
Tel: (860) 354-7651

Oliver Konig
Wimberly Allison Tong & Goo
2222 Kalakaua Avenue, Penthouse
Honolulu, Hawaii 96815
Tel: (808) 922-1253
Fax: (808) 931-1692

Ray Mains
Wailea Resort Company, Ltd.
161 Wailea Ike Place
Wailea, Kihei, Hawaii 96753
Tel: (808) 879-4465
Fax: (808) 874-0150

Milroy & McAleer
711 West 17th Street, #6107
Costa Mesa, California 92627
Tel: (714) 722-6402
Fax: (714) 722-6371

Ron Mitchell
Wimberly Allison Tong & Goo
2222 Kalakaua Avenue, Penthouse
Honolulu, Hawaii 96815
Tel: (808) 922-1253
Fax: (808) 931-1692

Andy Newman
Carnival Cruise Lines
3655 NW 87 Avenue
Miami, Florida 33178
Tel: (305) 599-2600
Fax: (305) 599-8630

Tom Ordway
Jean-Michel Cousteau Productions
1933 Cliff Drive #4
Santa Barbara, California 93109
Tel: (805) 899-8899
Fax: (805) 899-8898

Peter Paige
269 Parkside Road
Harrington Park, New Jersey 07640
Tel: (201) 767-3150
Fax: (201) 767-9263

R. Greg Hursley, Inc.
4003 Cloudy Ridge
Austin, Texas 78734
Tel: (512) 266-1391
Fax: (512) 266-1392

Kyle Rothenberg
2559 Ipulei Way
Honolulu, Hawaii 96816
Tel: (808) 523-1000

Mark Surloff
1655 NE 115th Street
Miami, Florida 33191
Tel: (305) 899-8450

Mike Wilson
7015 San Mateo Boulevard
Dallas, Texas 75223
Tel: (214) 328-8627

Frank Zimmerman
P. O. Box 709 - Madison Square Station
New York, New York 10159
Tel: (212) 532-8102

Index

PHOTOGRAPHERS

Acknowledgments

The publication of this book would have been impossible without the international roster of owners, operators, interior designers, and landscape architects who not only brought the facilities on these pages to life but also allowed us to include them in this volume. Equally crucial to our work on this book was discovering the images that really tell the story, and great appreciation is extended to the photographers who brilliantly captured the spirit and design details of each property represented here.

Consummate professionals to whom we extend special kudos for sharing with us their expertise about the travel, tourism, and design industries are: Pam Blanton (Aspen Skiing Company); Frances Borden (Frances Borden Public Relations); Connie Campbell (Wilson & Associates); Mazeppa Costa (Wimberly Allison Tong & Goo); Karyn Millet (Victoria King Public Relations); Mark Milroy and Mary McAleer (Milroy & McAleer); and Stacy Udell (Middleton & Gendron).

A deep debt of gratitude is due Kevin Clark of The Design Consultancy for his expert professional guidance in the fields of interior design and book publishing. It was Mr. Clark who brought us to the attention of PBC International's Penny Sibal and started the ball rolling on this and other projects.

Finally, we thank the accomplished entrepreneur and hotelier Adriana Mnuchin, owner with her husband, Robert, of the Mayflower Inn in Washington, Connecticut, for graciously accepting our invitation to provide the foreword to this volume. Her comments are as crisp and on the mark as her inn's decor and service.

John P. Radulski
William Weathersby, Jr.